Praise for The Hard W

"Although primarily a mountain climber,
outdoorsman and his life work should be of
has been tired, wet, cold, and hungry by their own design."

—St. Petersburg Times

"Fast paced . . . The Hard Way is written for both the hard-core 'been there, done that' crowd and those who would rather just read about it."

—Rocky Mountain News

"Jenkins, sometimes playfully and always entertainingly, describes his numerous brushes with the wilderness gods and how he has managed to walk, limp, and crawl away from his adventures."

—The Salt Lake Tribune

"Rich with adventure and intrigue . . . The intelligent, thoughtful, introspective side of Jenkins emerges from seemingly impossible situations during his travels around the globe."

—The Deseret News

The
Hard
Way

Mark Jenkins

Simon & Schuster Paperbacks

NEW YORK   LONDON   TORONTO   SYDNEY

SIMON & SCHUSTER PAPERBACKS
Rockefeller Center
1230 Avenue of the Americas
New York, NY 10020

First Simon & Schuster paperback edition 2003

SIMON & SCHUSTER PAPERBACKS and colophon are registered trademarks
of Simon & Schuster, Inc.

For information about special discounts for bulk purchases,
please contact Simon & Schuster Special Sales:
1-800-456-6798 or business@simonandschuster.com.

Designed by Paul Dippolito

Manufactured in the United States of America

3   5   7   9   10   8   6   4   2

The Library of Congress has cataloged the hardcover edition as follows:

Jenkins, Mark.
    The hard way / Mark Jenkins.
      p. cm.
      1. Outdoor recreation.   2. Jenkins, Mark.   I. Title.
    GV191.25 .J46 2002
    796.5—dc21   2002017615

ISBN-13: 978-0-7432-2227-3
ISBN-10:   0-7432-2227-X
ISBN-13: 978-0-7432-4941-6 (Pbk)
ISBN-10:   0-7432-4941-0 (Pbk)

The stories in this collection, often with different titles, were originally published in the following:

Outside, The Hard Way column: "What Goes Around," "Between the Wars," "Hitching," "The Bear," "Going to Hell," "Crossing to Safety," "Endangered Species," "Pickles," "In the Good Company of the Dead," "Once a Phantom," "Thin Ice," "Somebody Else's Rum," "Tombstone White," "Ego Trip," "Breathless Heights," "McKinley Redux," "He Ain't Heavy," "From the Mouths of Babes."

GQ: "Pulling Your Own Weight," "Running Stairs."

Bicycling: "The Bike Messenger."

Sports Afield: "The Snowcave," "A Mere Flesh Wound."

For my daughters, *Addi* and *Teal*—
who are the greatest adventure of my life.

Contents

To head toward a star—this only.

—Martin Heidegger

Prologue

I am leaving for Afghanistan. There isn't much time to prepare, but then there never is. I'm barely back from the last trip; I e-mailed the story at four this morning. Now. Buy another ticket, reload the pack, go.

I ordered the Defense Department maps a month ago. Five foot square, 1:500,000 topographic tactical pilotage charts, the disclaimer printed in bold: *Aircraft infringing upon non–free flying territory may be fired on without warning.*

Maps are essential. Planning a journey without a map is like building a house without drawings. It's hard to know where you're going if you don't know where you are. Since a boy, I've been diving into maps as if they were secret ponds in the forest. The first story I ever sold was about map and compass navigation. About how we find our way through the landscape. I'm still writing about that. Still getting lost.

I've been reading the history. The stream of spies that Britain began trickling into the country as far back as 1810. The forty-seven British military expeditions, every one of which failed. The Russian generals repeatedly sent to conquer the inconquerable desert kingdom–cum–graveyard. The intrigues of American imperialism. The CIA, the KGB, Pakistan's ISI, Afghanistan's KHAD, the mujahedin, the jihad, the madrassas. The endless succession of fractious warlords who butcher their own people almost as often as the enemy. It's hard to know where things are going if you don't know where things have been.

The expander file is overflowing with news clippings, obscure U.N. reports, development agency white papers, etc. I read them all. I read the footnotes and the appendixes; these are the primary sources, authored by experts, some of whom might be worth talking to.

This is homework, something I do for every assignment. Most of it will never appear in the story. It's like the foundation of a house. You don't see it, but without it, the house would collapse.

Why Afghanistan? Because it fascinates me. As do Burma, Ethiopia, Bolivia, Tibet, Turkey, Greece, Holland—all for different reasons. It has always been this way. I cannot get enough of the world. To smell it, walk through it, sink the teeth of my mind into it. I am not a writer who began writing at the age of eight in a little room at a little desk and dreamed of being a novelist. At eight I was flying on a bicycle through the pungent sagebrush in the red hills beyond the edge of town.

My first real job I worked on a dirt-dry ranch running sheep. Breakfast at five A.M., dinner at nine P.M., dollar an hour. I was twelve. When I was thirteen my family moved from the snow-drifted plains of Wyoming to the fecund polders of Holland. My father, a mathematics professor, had a sabbatical. Mom put all six kids directly into Dutch schools. We were bilingual in a matter of months. Europe—its complex history and vast literature and cosmopolitan perspective— was poured into us as if we were empty vessels. After a year we returned to Wyoming, infected. Wanderlust is incurable.

I lied about my age, fabricated a Social Security number, and got a job with the Union Pacific. I worked on a tie gang as a gandy dancer and slept in a boxcar with the Navajo up at Fox Park. The next summer I worked on a rail gang and slept in a tent behind the Virginian Hotel in Medicine Bow. The next summer I worked on a drilling rig out in the Red Desert. Almost through high school, money in my pocket, itching to see the world, I lit out.

My passport, richly tattooed, already has the Afghanistan visa and I have managed to obtain several letters of introduction. Little pieces of paper to prove that we are who we say we are when in fact forging these documents is cheap and easy. I've done it.

My vaccination record has been stamped and signed so many times it's falling apart. Cholera, hepatitis, meningitis, tetanus, diphtheria, yellow fever, polio, typhoid, measles, mumps, rubella. You need only become deathly ill once, deep inside some festering, forgotten jungle, to look forward to needles.

Write another last-minute list.

The bank for a bundle of cash—credit cards and traveler's checks being meaningless where I'm bound. Patch the hole in the two-man tent, recoat the hiking boots, get iodine crystals from the chemistry lab for sterilizing water. Buy one more notebook: the antiquated pen and paper are still the remote writer's tools, light, abusable, no electricity needed. Film for the Nikon—a camera is like a travel companion, it keeps one's memory honest. Spare batteries for the headlamp. You never know when you will have to move at night.

Anxiety is building now. The footloose jubilation of setting out on a new adventure masking the anguish of saying goodbye to my wife and two daughters. This is the conundrum of my life: I do not want to leave, but I am yearning, madly, to go.

The plane is waiting. Shoulder the pack, kiss Sue and the girls, I'm gone.

CROSSINGS

What Goes Around

I killed the rat. Even though the woman who swept the courtyard told me I would bring bad karma upon myself. The rat was menacing the bunk room. It was an oily sewer rat. Every night it crept into the room after we were asleep and clawed into our backpacks, gorging itself on our extra food. One night it leapt onto the face of a Danish girl and got its claws tangled in her long blond hair and she woke up screaming. Enough is enough.

The Tibetan woman who swept the stone courtyard wore a traditional gown, trim and dark, and plaited her raven hair into a thick braid. She was slight and beautiful. She came from a remote village and was a devout Buddhist. She looked into my face and told me no one sold rat traps in Lhasa. In the market I found almost everyone sold heavy, serrated, spring-loaded metal rat traps. I bought one and baited it with a cube of yak meat and placed it under my bunk. I heard the loud snap around midnight, desperate thumping, a final jerk. I pulled my sleeping bag over my head and slept soundly.

In the morning the woman was solemn and anxious, but the other travelers staying in the bunk room were relieved. Killing the rat is how I became friends with Maury and Brigitte.

"Thanks," said Brigitte. "No one else would have done it."

"I know I wouldn't have," said Maury.

Brigitte was a Canadian physics student and a climber with round, light blue doll's eyes. Her name was pronounced *Brrigeet*. She was traveling alone. She carried her Tibetan phrase book everywhere she went and despite all the laughter she provoked, she was actually learning Tibetan. She would eventually return to Canada to ace her undergraduate work and be invited to Geneva to earn her Ph.D.

Maury, a tall, beach-blond Aussie and former lifeguard, was an itinerant carpenter currently hailing from Vancouver, who built decks half the year and traveled the other half. He loved to dive and knew every brilliant blue-water lagoon from Honduras to Hong Kong.

That evening, with a ratless night to look forward to, Maury and Brigitte and I went out together to celebrate. On the way to the restaurant Maury bought a case of bottled beer and carried it lightly on his shoulder. We laughed so hard and stayed out so late we were locked out and had to pound on the great wooden gate to get in.

The next day, hanging out in the courtyard in the cold sunshine, I asked each of them if they were up for something illegal.

"What do you think, mate?" said Maury, breaking into his habitual smile.

"Always," said Brigitte. I didn't know if this was true or not.

I wanted to go to Lhamo Latso, the holiest lake in Tibet. I'd been hearing about the lake since my first journey to Tibet in 1984. In the slums of Delhi, where the beggar children with limbs broken backward by their parents peer up from the ground, I had found a book titled The Power-Places of Central Tibet for sale, hiding between an Indian tome on sexual positions and a photo biography of the Beatles. In it there was a description of Lhamo Latso: "It is a Tibetan belief older than Buddhism that every individual, every family, and an entire country, possesses a 'life-spirit,' called la. This la is embodied in natural phenomena, such as mountains, lakes, trees and so on. When the place of residence of the la is damaged, the individual, family or nation suffers directly. Thus when a lake that is the home of the la dries up, this omen of death or disaster can inflict the terrible result that is presaged. The life-spirit of Tibet is identified with Lhamo Latso."

Lhamo Latso is also the geographical life-spirit for all Dalai Lamas. It is a surprisingly small lake, a tiny oval barely recognizable on a map, located a hundred miles southeast of Lhasa near the head of the

Metoktang Valley. Over the centuries, most Dalai Lamas made a pilgrimage to this oracle. By staring into its cold, lapping waters each Dalai Lama could divine essential clues to who his reincarnation would be. When the thirteenth Dalai Lama died suddenly in 1935, the Regent of Tibet made a pilgrimage to Lhamo Latso, where, transfixed by the turquoise water, he had a vision that gave exact details for finding his spiritual leader's reincarnation, Tenzin Gyatso, the fourteenth (and current) Dalai Lama—a heretofore unknown two-year-old boy living in a lost yak-dung village in central Tibet.

I had food, tents, and camping gear left over from an aborted expedition, but neither Maury nor Brigitte had come to Tibet prepared to live out in the cold, so we went shopping. In lieu of a Chinese army slicker Maury thought too expensive, he bought himself an enormous white plastic gunnysack. We cut out holes for his head and arms, and he pulled it on and tied a rope around his waist.

"You look like a priest from the Middle Ages," cried Brigitte, delighted.

"You know it gets cold above 15,000 feet," I warned.

"No drama," said Maury—Aussie for "don't worry"—and donned a green felt fedora he'd purchased instead of a Tibetan sheepskin cap.

Brigitte borrowed my fleece long underwear and bought herself a Tibetan scarf and a floppy wool cap. She would stay swaddled in them for the next two weeks.

The Chinese were requiring foreigners to hire a guide, a driver, and a jeep and to obtain (i.e., buy) three or four permits for any travel outside Lhasa. We couldn't have received permission to go to Lhamo Latso in any case; it was deep inside an off-limits chunk of Tibet the size of Texas, and four days of hard mountain hiking from the nearest road.

We snuck out of town before dawn, catching a lift on a local bus overloaded with Tibetans bundled up like Inuit, the bus driver eyeing us in a shard of mirror. We hid under the seats at the police roadblocks. Where the bus U-turned we jumped out and started walking away fast, not looking back, not turning around, expecting to be stopped and questioned and perhaps jailed, but it didn't happen. We negotiated a ride with a well-connected local, sardined into the back of his jeep, and he drove us straight through every dusty roadblock with a grin and a wave.

At dusk the jeep dropped us near the mouth of the Metoktang Valley. We slipped across the Tsangpo River on a tank-wide suspension bridge that was inexplicably unguarded, hiked up into the canyon, and pitched camp in a muddy field encircled by apricot trees. I couldn't believe how lucky we'd been. Lying in my bag, I must have said so out loud.

"No such thing, mate," whispered Maury from the other tent. Brigitte was already curled up asleep beside me.

"What's that?"

"No such thing as luck."

In the morning, mist wreathed the valley. To either side, treeless slopes reared up a mile in the sky. We walked the hard-frozen track in the shade and watched the sunlight coming for us like castaways watch an approaching ship. When the light finally sailed into the bottom of the valley, the temperature leapt fifty degrees. In minutes winter metamorphosed into summer. The river began to cough and jerk and then run free, the pastures turned from frost-white to green, and shouting shepherd kids sprouted on the hillsides. That's how the world works above 15,000 feet. Of course, it could just as easily have been snowing.

"So, Maury," I said. "You don't believe in luck?"

He had his pants hiked up, revealing the funny laceless, ankle-length boots called Blundstones that Aussies are partial to. He'd taken off his fedora and was strolling hat in hand. "Luck isn't something you *can* believe in," he said. "Luck is the word used by people who don't believe."

"Good things happen and it's not just a matter of luck?"

"Nope. They were supposed to happen."

"And bad things?"

"Same." Maury was practicing twirling his fedora on the tip of his finger and catching it. "Everything happens for a reason, Mark."

Brigitte was just ahead, practically skipping even with a heavy pack. Like Maury, she was implacably gay. You couldn't get either of them to say a bad word about anything or anybody if you tortured them.

"So you must believe in karma."

"I do."

"And reincarnation."

"They go together." Maury flashed a smile and flipped the fedora up into the air. It made several slow circles and landed perfectly on his head.

To me, it seemed like the oddest coincidence that I should wind up walking to Lhamo Latso with a man who actually believed in reincarnation. But then Maury would have said that that's because it wasn't a coincidence at all.

That night we camped in the bleak medieval village of Tseqgu. Brigitte danced among the snot-faced urchins practicing her Tibetan until they clutched our fingers with their dirt-blackened hands and pulled us into the squalor of a stone hut. We had to stoop and could see almost nothing in the tenebrous light. We were led through a wooden fence separating the goats and sheep from the humans but allowing the animals' body heat to half-warm the cramped black space. An old man plunging a yak butter churn greeted us with gnarled hands and invited us to sit on a dirt bench beside a glowing hearth. Small steaming potatoes were poured into a basket on the floor. The children squatted on their haunches, wiped the green mucus from their faces, and we all ate together.

The next morning there were three inches of snow on the ground. While we were packing up the tents a shivering, barefoot boy, ragged and filthy, passed by carrying a heavy water jug. I looked at Maury.

"OKay, mate, if it's bothering you so much, this is what I believe: Every thought, every word, every action produces karma. Our karma carries on from life to life. It's a spiritual progression. Bit by bit, act by act, life after life, we create our own karma. Acts of kindness in this life beget gifts of kindness in the next. Acts of cruelty in this life beget suffering in the next. It's self-fulfilling retribution and reward. It's a spiritual quest for learning, and we all have a choice as to what path we will take."

Brigitte asked Maury how the actions of others affected an individual's karma.

"Depends on how you respond," he said. "It's up to you."

In the honey light of late afternoon we reached the forlorn but still magnificent Chokorgyel Monastery. Chokorgyel was built in one of the ancient geomantic hot spots of Tibet—a vast triangular plain at the confluence of three rivers and surrounded by three mountains symbolizing the perfect harmony of three elements: earth, water, and air. The monastery's castlelike walls form an equilateral triangle, a quarter mile to a side. Gendun Gyatso, the second Dalai Lama, founded the monastery in 1509 as a place of rest and worship for all those making the pilgrimage to Lhamo Latso.

We popped up the tents outside the walls of the monastery across from the black wool tents of the Tibetan nomads. Lion-dogs—immense mastiffs with the solid bodies of rottweilers but the matted coat and lion ruffs of chows—were staked outside these tents barking themselves hoarse.

The Chokorgyel Monastery, or gompa, was razed by the Dzungar

Mongols in 1718, rebuilt, then destroyed again by the Chinese in 1959. Inside the walls were the beheaded skeletons of hundreds of stone buildings, including several temples. Before the tanks and dynamite, there were 500 monks at Chokorgyel; now, we discovered, there were only two: an old man and a young man living amidst the ruins, quiet and transparent as spirits. They thought we were pilgrims—and we were, although I didn't know it then. To reach Lhamo Latso, they told us, follow the wide stone path leading northeast from the monastery. We would find the way.

The lion-dogs barked all night, lunging and snapping taut their heavy chains, mistaking attacks of wind for intruders. We collapsed the tents in the predawn dark and dragged them through the huge wooden gates, leaving them on the broken stones of the former temple as the monks had suggested. Slipping back out below a whistling sky, we moved along the wall past the piles of stone tablets all engraved with the same hypnotic chant—om mani padme hum, om mani padme hum, om mani padme hum, "hail to the jewel in the lotus"—as if the wind itself were using the tablets as a hymnal.

To stay warm, we hiked swiftly. By the time we crossed the Metoktang River it was light enough to switch off the headlamps. The monks had told us Lhamo Latso was a four-hour walk from Chokorgyel. When we reached a cluster of cairns, we were to turn due north, passing through a yak herder's camp.

The cairns were covered with snow. In the camp there were great black yaks snorting columns of white steam and a woman in angular swaths of black fabric milking a yak with a red bell. Brigitte went over to speak with her, but the woman fled to her black tent.

It was steep going up into a hanging valley and then level again. Cold squalls kept coming and going. I was making my case for the irrationality of reincarnation and waiting for Brigitte, the scientist, the physicist, to chime in.

"Matter cannot be created or destroyed, only re-formed," she said at last. "I guess I don't see why it should be that different for the spirit."

"Brigitte!"

"Well, Mark, I don't."

Maury was walking ahead of us with his arms crossed, his hands inside his sleeves, and his fedora pulled down over his ears. "We not only come back in a new form," he said. "I believe we choose the form we come back in."

"What!" This was too much. "Who would ever choose to come back as that dying, barefoot child we saw carrying water yesterday morning?"

"I don't know," said Maury, his tone implying not that it couldn't happen, but that he himself didn't have an answer.

"C'mon Maury, this is preposterous. Forget about coming back as a beetle or a rat; just take a child who dies of starvation or AIDS or malaria. Who would choose that life? For that matter, take any kid who is abused by his parents and tell me he chose to be reincarnated into that kind of suffering."

Maury glanced back over his shoulder. "I suppose it depends on the kind of lives, the hundreds or thousand of lives he's lived before."

It was too cold to talk anymore. We eventually reached the 17,300-foot pass overlooking Lhamo Latso, "a sharp cragged ridge," according to *The Power-Places of Central Tibet*, "upon which is built the Dalai Lama's throne, and from this eminence the divine rulers of Tibet once sat to gaze into the lake . . . to divine the future." The throne was buried beneath untold thousands of prayer flags frozen into an icy mound, and the wind was cutting us in half. The sacred lake was a blue mirror set down inside a ring of mountains. It didn't look sacred. It looked just like a thousand other inhospitable high-altitude tarns found everywhere in Tibet.

Maury and Brigitte and I tried to stay up high and stare down into the oracle-lake because we all want a vision, we all want something mysterious and inexplicable and full of portent to happen to us—especially those of us who doubt such things can happen. We braced ourselves amid the creaking flags and peered down into the hard blue lake until our eyes blurred and our faces froze and our feet began to slip. To me it was just like standing on the summit of a mountain: no divination, no enlightenment, just the howl and bite of cold doing all it could to freeze solid the blood in three beating hearts.

That night bullets of snow strafed our tents and the lion-dogs yelped and the monastery stood silent as stone. The next day we crossed Gyelong Pass in a whiteout, the tower of prayer flags on top guiding us like a lighthouse. The day after that we woke to eight inches of snow, and more falling.

By now we'd each settled into our roles, which of course were not roles at all but who we really were, so there was harmony. I was the navigator, plotting our course over the earth and through the mountains on small-scale, declassified military maps, reading between the brown lines. Brigitte was the bubbly, fluid linguist who got us invited in for boiled potatoes and yak butter tea by every Tibetan home or tent we came near. And Maury was the incorrigible optimist, the man who quipped merrily no matter how deep the snow or how hungry we were, even when it got so cold we were forced to cram into one tent and sleep in a pile to keep from freezing to death.

One evening we followed a mule cart stacked high with hay into the village of Woka Taktse. There was a dirt road trickling out of this village and a jeep for hire, and so our journey would end. The Tibetan women in their bright blue tunics and heavy wool aprons were on the flat roofs of their mud homes, beating stalks of barley and singing softly in the twilight.

Brigitte the pied piper was ahead, surrounded by a pack of jubilant urchins. Maury and I were sauntering side by side talking. I was telling him how lucky I was to have been raised in a big family where everyone was loved.

"No such thing."

"Love?"

Maury hooted. "Luck, mate. Luck!"

"What about you, Maury? What was your family like?"

"Ah, well . . ."

"Well what?"

"It was a learning experience."

"What's that mean?"

Brigitte was now being led by the hand of a bowlegged old woman. It was almost dark but the air was still warm. Maury doffed his fedora and ran a hand through his scarecrow hair and told me that he had lived in terror as a boy because his father was a drunk. A mean-spirited drunk who all through Maury's childhood beat him and his mother.

Between the Wars

We beach beside a pillbox that has fallen into the water. We've seen many of them along the coast of Gallipoli. Blocks of concrete with walls four feet thick and one deep hole for the muzzle of the machine gun. They are from World War II, not World War I, but still the waves have worn away the sand beneath them and they have tumbled like boulders into the turquoise sea.

Jon and I step from the boat and drag it up out of the surf, our thighs pushing against the warm water. On the beach we change into dry shoes and set off climbing. The brine dries white on our dark faces and arms.

It is rough country, like much of western Turkey. A tangle of gulches and bluffs, the brush like bales of barbed wire. Most of the trenches of 1915 have caved in and disappeared but we occasionally find troughs that contour left or right. In these the ferocity and fear are still palpable. It is impossible to tell if they were Turkish or Allied trenches, or frontline trenches separated by only seven or eight yards and thus changed hands over and over until the no-man's-land was piled so high with the dead that a night's truce was called and the mounds cleared away under the starlight to make room for more slaughter in the morning.

There are small graveyards everywhere, hundreds of them, simple plots chopped from the quilled brush and leveled. We walk from one graveyard to the next on goat trails beneath a gleamy Aegean sky, rarely speaking. It is difficult to find something to say that means anything. Unlike on other battlefields, here the men were buried together, with their comrades, where they fell.

The sign outside one cemetery: HERE WERE BURIED 378 SOLDIERS, SAILORS AND MARINES OF THE BRITISH EMPIRE WHO DIED ON THE GALLIPOLI PENINSULA. OF THESE, THE GRAVES OF 359 ARE KNOWN.

We move through the headstones.

379 Trooper

E.C. Bell

3rd Australian Light Horse

19 May 1915, Age 22

**Loving husband of Nellie, beloved father
of Eva, Dulcie and Erica**

335 Trooper

W.J. Monaghan

1st Australian Light Horse

29 June 1915, Age 25

**Loved brother of Peter, Ferg,
Ignot and Mollie**

Plaque after small plaque, row after row, filling cemetery after cemetery as orderly as they stood up from their trenches and charged into certain, tautological death. It is irreconcilable. It takes us hours, working our way from the beachhead up the implausible ridges, battlefield to battlefield. Hell Spit, Shrapnel Valley, Plugge's Plateau, Russell's Top, the Nek, Baby 700. After a while it becomes almost too much.

"You'd think they would have at least tried a flanking maneuver."

"I would have thought," replies Jon, "after 100,000 casualties, they would have tried any other maneuver whatsoever."

We circle back down to the boat, passing through the equally crowded Turkish cemeteries.

Between the orders to attack and die, orders that came from men whom the soldiers never saw and thus could never respect, gifts were tossed back and forth. The Turks would loft over tomatoes or figs, the Allied soldiers pitch back grenades of bully beef and cigarettes. The Turks were marched to Gallipoli to defend their homeland from infidel invaders; the English and Aussies and New Zealanders shipped to Turkey to defeat the barbarians who had joined the German invaders. And after they had watched each other die, as young men die, heroically and terrorized and pinioned by the unspeakable absurdity, bodies torn through and flopped into the dirt, after they had heard men crying for help and then nothing, this propaganda vanished and they became strange blood brothers whom fate had pitted against each other and thus they would kill, but not hate.

There is a graveyard in the cove where we left the kayak. It is called Anzac Cove ("Anzac" the acronym for Australian and New Zealand Allied Corps). Some of the most futile, most inhuman fighting in the history of man took place here between April 25, 1915, and January 8, 1916, when the last British-led troops departed. This is the inscription carved into the stone monument:

> There is no difference between the Johnnies and the Mehmets to us where they lie side by side here in this country of ours. You the mothers who sent your sons from faraway countries, wipe away your tears; your sons are now lying in our bosom and are in peace. After having lost their lives on this land, they have become our sons as well.
>
> —Mustafa Kemal

We are sea-kayaking through history. It is why we came to Turkey. My partner is a big man from Casper, Wyoming, named Jon Huss. Jon, forty-three, is a civil attorney in the midst of an extended sabbatical devoted almost entirely to adventure. I had called him at the suggestion of an astute neighbor who said, cryptically, "Jon is the guy for this journey." We'd never met.

"I want to kayak down the Dardanelles, circle the Gallipoli peninsula, then cross over to Troy," I said when I called him. "I have no idea if it's possible. You want to go?"

The Strait of Dardanelles is that improbably thin channel that cleaves Asia from Europe. Forty miles long, varying in width from four miles to less than a mile, it is Turkey's natural Panama Canal. The Black Sea pours south through the Bosphorus into the Sea of Marmara; the Sea of Marmara empties via the Dardanelles Strait into the Aegean. The Aegean becomes the Mediterranean and the Mediterranean is a portal to the planet.

Slaves to silk, oil to automobiles, the Dardanelles has been one of the most important shipping lanes on earth since there were ships. Which makes it strategic. Which makes it the site of one war after another for the last 3,000 years. Troy, scene of one of the greatest tragedies, or triumphs, of ancient history, lies at the mouth of the Dardanelles in Asia. The Gallipoli peninsula, scene of one of the greatest tragedies, or triumphs, of the twentieth century, lies in Europe, four miles across the strait.

"The Hellespont. That's what the ancient Greeks called it," responded Jon. "It's where Xerxes, the Persian general, built a bridge of boats and marched across an army of two million to invade Greece and conquer Athens. But the Athenians were defending their homeland, and they routed the Persians at the battle of Salamis."

Jon had read Herodotus's *The Histories* in Greek. One of his favorite books from boyhood was Schliemann's *Troy and Its Remains*. He also happened to be a veteran boater.

I was leaving in seventy-two hours. Jon rang back in two to say that he'd booked his ticket. We flew to Istanbul and bused south to Gelibolu, a fishing port near the top of the Dardanelles on the European side. We assembled the skin-and-ribs, two-hole kayak in the town square and a crowd carried the craft to the water.

I'd read that there was an implacable four-knot current gushing down the Dardanelles. During World War I an Allied submarine had been trapped in one of its eddies, located by a German spotting plane, and shelled into oblivion. Gales had shattered boats a hundred times the size of ours on the rocky shores. The wind sometimes blew fifty knots down the channel.

"We'll find out," said Jon.

Six-foot-four and still built like the rower he had been at the University of Pennsylvania, Jon sat in the bow. He was the self-described "hammer." A mere five-foot-eight, I sat in the stern as the helmsman. We clicked paddles only a few times before hitting a rhythm that would last the whole trip.

Down the center of the strait was the two-way traffic of the colossal cargo ships. We were in the seafaring equivalent of a bike lane. We stayed well to the right of the channel, but still, whenever one of these behemoths plowed past, two minutes later a three-foot wake would hurl us sideways.

Paddling hard, assisted by the ferocious tailwind and strong current, we could sometimes outpace sailboats. One afternoon, caught up in the joy of skipping over the water, we inadvertently veered into the shipping lane. A supertanker, bulldozing down right behind us, blasted her bullhorn and sent us hightailing it back toward the shoreline. In the Narrows, the most constricted part of the strait, where the water is funneled in tight and practically roars, we found ourselves, as Jon put it, "surfing the banana"—shooting our frumpy, too-flexible vessel down the faces of waves.

We ran the Dardanelles in three days.

But rounding the horn and coming back up the peninsula was a different story. The wind and current, once our allies, became our enemies. Together they pushed us too far offshore, where we battled six- to eight-foot swells. Jon never changed his calm, steady stroke. He would turn his head just before he was smacked in the face with a wave. Sometimes our aluminum-boned boat would get high-centered and make a horrible cracking sound. Once, when the kayak groaned and then shrieked as if it were about to break in two, Jon laconically suggested, "You might want to bring 'er a little closer to shore."

The boating was great sport, but it was also something more. The history of the Dardanelles is a maritime epic. Every battle ever fought here was fought over control of the seaway. Every war a war over who would control the water. It was fitting to explore such history by boat. The scars on the land had largely healed, but the sea was still the same sea, the same dispassionate, incandescent blue liquid all the soldiers had seen and smelled and touched. Several times a day we pulled up onto a famous beachhead and hiked off to a battlefield or monument to take another class in the classical history of war.

It turns out the entire Gallipoli campaign—directed by Winston Churchill, then Britain's First Lord of the Admiralty—was one massive flanking maneuver, an attempt to slip around the Western Front and come in behind the Germans. Force the Dardanelles, take Constantinople, push on through to the Black Sea to reinforce the Russians, creating a true Eastern Front. On paper it was a good plan. It might have put an early end to World War I and saved hundreds of thousands of lives. That is, if the British generals sent to Gallipoli had not been incompetent, cowardly, and incomprehendably indecisive. If communications had been better. If the Turks hadn't been so willing to die for their country. If an unknown commander named Kemal Mustafa— later to become Ataturk, father of modern Turkey, their George Washington, his bust in every village—hadn't been so ruthless and so right. Instead, the Gallipoli campaign was an Allied disaster in which some 50,000 soldiers were killed and more than 200,000 wounded.

Two thousand five hundred years earlier, Xerxes had underestimated the Greeks just as the Brits had underestimated the Turks, with the same bloody result. History is the reiteration of history. Only the names change.

Churchill, discredited and nearly disgraced, was demoted and sent to fight on the Western Front. It would take him two decades to battle his way back to Prime Minister. He would use what he learned at Gallipoli to make the invasion of Normandy, in World War II, a stunning success.

But Gallipoli was a tragedy only to the losers. To the Turks, it was the beginning of their war of independence against foreign domination, the birth pangs of the modern Turkish state.

After a week of boating from one tough lesson to the next in Europe—from Cape Helles and Y Beach to Anzac Cove and Sulva Bay—it was time to go to Asia.

To traverse the strait we couldn't cut directly across the mouth; the current is so strong we would have been pushed out to sea. Studying the charts, we decided to paddle back up the western coastline for three miles, then strike out at an acute angle to the flow.

We stayed out of the main channel, weaving through the islands of rock close to shore. Our arms worked the soft water along the edges while our eyes watched the freighters churning up and down the Dardanelles, trying to gauge their speed and pick a moment to shoot through a gap in the traffic.

When the time came we swept out and the current caught us and we paddled with purpose, slicing off the tops of the waves. Ten minutes later, with ocean to burn, we made it across the path of a Russian container ship heading south. But the median was a quarter-mile wide. By the time we reached the northbound traffic lane, there was another ship charging up the strait. I didn't alter our bearing.

"I'd say," said Jon, turning around to look at me, "that we're on a collision course."

"I think we can make it."

The ship was coming up fast, but I still thought we were going to pull it off and just slip by, when suddenly the ship was almost above us. Frothy white waves were curling back from the enormous prow. I slammed the rudder and the boat peeled hard to starboard.

"Thank you," said Jon, as we watched the leviathan pass to port and braced for the wake.

After another ten minutes, surfing every fifth crest, we reached Asia, beaching beside a military installation at the mouth of the Dardanelles. Too late we noticed the barbed wire and guards in towers and giant concrete bulwarks set in the sea with warnings painted in Turkish in big red letters. The moment we stood up—drenched from head to toe, with our bare hairy legs and droopy spray skirts making us look like two ballerinas in drag—the whistles started blowing. The men in the guard towers were waving their machine guns at us. We tried stepping left or right to appease them but they kept frantically blowing their whistles and waving their weapons. We stayed right where we were.

Eventually a mustachioed commander, escorted by several soldiers, came out to have a little talk with us. He had an interpreter. He wanted to know what the hell we thought we were doing. We told him we were just boating. Just tourists. He studied us, two drippy guys with goofy grins. He studied our unconventional spy boat.

"Can you read that!" The commander and his interpreter pointed to the big red letters on the concrete embankment.

We shook our heads like two kids in first grade.

"That says, 'It is prohibited to come within 600 meters of this post.' If you come within 600 meters you will be fired upon. Do you know where you are?"

We shook our heads again.

"You are at zero meters!" The commander smiled. "Now," the interpreter translated, "are you hungry?"

Two soldiers carrying metal trays came striding out to the beach. Lentils in hamburger gravy, yogurt with strips of cucumber, feta torte, a pear, bread, a metal pitcher of water. We were enjoined to eat.

The commander wanted to know our plans.

"We're on our way to Troy," said Jon.

After lunch the commander told us to leave the kayak right where it was and he escorted us through the gates of his fortress, Jon and I looking askance at all the ordnance. We were taken to a jeep, given a lift to a village just outside the site of ancient Troy, and told to be back at five P.M. for a return ride to the base.

Troy is one fortress built upon the ruins of a past fortress, built upon the ruins of a past fortress . . . going back 5,000 years. There is a huge wooden replica of the Trojan Horse at the entrance. Remember the *Iliad*? The Trojans are tricked into believing that the wooden horse left by the apparently defeated and departing Greeks is honestly a gift to their gods, and they wheel it right through the gates. Of course the stallion contains warriors who slip out of its belly that night, signal their waiting comrades by setting fire to the city, retrieve the beautiful queen Helen, and win the war. According to Homer, a Greek.

Our scheduled ride appeared and we were driven back through the checkpoints. We said our farewells and walked right through the heart of the base and out the other side to our sea horse.

That evening we stroke up the Dardanelles into dusk. The sky and the water move past through curtains of purple. Just as it gets too dark to continue, a tiny harbor appears. We slide in through the seawalls. There is no village here, just a silent collection of small fishing boats. We are hailed in the dark, the voice coming across the black water.

We paddle over to find five old men sitting in the stern of a tiny vessel. They are sweaty and unshaven, joking softly with one another, sharing dinner together. They tie our boat to theirs and pull us into their company. They squeeze together to make room and the boat rocks. The swaying light bulb illuminates their creased, sunburned faces like a campfire. Again Jon and I are fed. We break out our ship-wreck rations: three tall cans of Troy beer. They want to know all about our voyage. We tell them the tale with the aid of a Turkish dictionary and arm movements that represent the water in its different moods. They nod knowingly. It turns out they are all retired sailors, all once officers in the Turkish navy. Now they are doing what old sailors do in the lucky, less heroic times of history: fishing. They sleep with their fat wives and slip out to their little boats at dawn, sometimes with a son or a niece, troll into the Dardanelles and fish all day and then gather together and eat the fish in the harbor in the night under the stars in a boat.

Until the next war.

The sailors ask where we are sleeping.

"Camping," says Jon, making a teepee with his fingers.

They guide us in the dark along the line of little boats along the stone wharf to the shore, where there is an invisible flat place to lie down, and say good night.

In the morning we will strike out up the Dardanelles. We will be paddling against a four-knot current into a twenty-knot headwind. There will be whitecaps crashing onto the bow. We will look over at the shore, and although we will be paddling with all our strength, we'll seem to be standing still. And yet, Jon and I will pass all the way up through the Narrows by noon. I too am mystified by this.

At dawn we wake to find that we have been sleeping beneath the barrel of a ten-inch cannon set inside a pillbox.

Hitching

Another car blows by. I drop my arm and fold in my thumb. The driver didn't even look at me. He was staring down the road as if there was something so interesting out there he couldn't take his eyes off it. It's a common response: I'll act like I don't see him so maybe he won't see me, so I won't have to think about him standing there in the cold while I fly right on by. The emperor's new clothes in reverse. I understand. Nobody likes to feel guilty.

Of course maybe he doesn't feel guilty at all. Maybe he thinks I'm getting what I deserve, for what kind of an American doesn't have a car? What in the world did I do to lose this great country's God-given right to automobile ownership. I must have done something. Decent Americans, even decent poor Americans, own a car and drive it everywhere. A man afoot in America is no man at all. A man afoot is a loser.

I wait. A freezing prairie wind is rattling the reflector poles. It's trying to snow again. Flakes cartwheel across the highway like tiny tumbleweeds.

A pickup comes around the curve. The driver is wearing a cowboy hat. I put out my thumb and look him in the eyes. He looks right back into mine. People believe if they look into your eyes they can discern the truth—for instance, whether I'm an ordinary guy down on my luck or a serial murderer. It's nonsense, but if you want a ride you play along. The cowboy stabs sideways with his finger, indicating he's turning off just up the road. I wave and he casually salutes as he passes.

The snow is coming now, brilliant white confetti tumbling all around. I should put on sunglasses but don't. Sunglasses make you look like you're trying to hide something. Your thoughts, your secrets, your identity. Sunglasses make you look unknown and people don't like the unknown.

A long, low-slung sedan shoots past. But then, in the corner of my eye, I catch the red glow of brake lights through the snowfall. I spin on my heels, run down the road, swing open the car door and get in.

Away we go.

There was a period in my life when I hitchhiked all over the country. The kind of car I could afford wouldn't have been reliable enough to go any distance, so I went without. I hitched from Wyoming to West 73rd in Manhattan to visit a friend. I hitched down to Tempe, Arizona, to see a girlfriend. I hitched out to Joshua Tree to go rock climbing. I hitched up to Boston to work for an uncle. Once, after a family reunion in Pennsylvania, I raced my own family back to Laramie. It was a gentleman's bet. Dad stopped on the highway, I got out, and he sped away with Mom and my five younger brothers and sisters staring out the rear window. It was 2,000 miles. I was sitting on our dusty porch, pretending to read the newspaper, when they drove up.

By then I'd learned that there's a right way and a wrong way to hitchhike. There are rules. The rules are based on human psychology, on generalizations about human behavior that are mostly true but sometimes gloriously or horribly false—which would account for how I once got a ride in Utah from a woman so beautiful and lonely I stepped onto the road the next morning without my belt, and likewise how I once got a lift in South Dakota from a hippie so hurting he held a cocked revolver against my temple for an hour.

Eventually I got a car and stopped hitchhiking. I wasn't a starving writer anymore, just a writer. When you own a car you own the world. You are invincible, invulnerable, free. Whenever I saw a hitchhiker I picked him up. I'd been there. Some of them had sorry tales, meant to elicit sympathy—stories that, even if counterfeit in every detail, were honest enough in spirit.

But over the years, hitchhiking got a bad name, the number of hitchhikers dwindled, and I began to wonder if hitchhiking was dying out. Fortunately, I'd recently received an invitation to a party in Santa Fe, New Mexico. I packed the rucksack, walked my kids to school, and asked my wife to drop me off at the edge of town. (Yes, she was upset about this potentially unhealthy exercise in investigative reporting.)

Rather than take I-25, which cleaves the plains from Wyoming south to New Mexico, I decided to thumb the blue highways down the spine of the Rockies. Fewer cars but fewer cops. Too many cars and everybody always thinks the next guy will pick you up. It was only about 600 miles, but given the current fear and loathing of hitchhikers, I figured I might be in for some long waits by the roadside. It was the dead of winter. I brought a sleeping bag.

My first ride was cheating. The driver was a friend.

"Mark! What in hell you doin' out there?" George said, flicking his cigarette out the window with the stumps of his thumb and fingers. He'd lost them in a sawmill accident. Dylan's *Blood on the Tracks* was playing on the tape deck.

"Little experiment."

George used to teach English at the university before things went sour. He told me a story about how he once hitchhiked up to Sheridan, Wyoming, with four Dostoyevsky novels and hid out in a motel just reading. "Finest damn week of my whole damn life," he declared. Then he talked about his divorce. He was trying to figure out how to get more time with his kids.

George dropped me off at the sawmill turnoff, twelve miles out of town. "Good luck, man. I wouldn't have picked you up if I didn't know you."

I didn't wait five minutes before the next car stopped. Country music on the radio. Driver's name was John. Thin black mustache, smoked discount cigarettes. A traveling salesman.

"Industrial parts. I used to be in-house sales. Then one day I couldn't take it anymore. I couldn't take one more minute being inside an office."

John was on his way to the lumber mill in Saratoga.

"They're my best customers, but the phone won't do the trick. They need to see a face."

At the mountains we disappeared into a blizzard, the snow swirling in from all directions. We slowed down to twenty miles an hour.

"Used to drive a truck," John said. "You don't take chances with snow. Nothing wrong with being a little late. Go off the road and you could be late forever."

Peering through the fogged windshield, I thought how grand it was to be inside, dry and warm and moving along, when I could just as easily have been outside, cold and wet and going nowhere.

John started to talk about his fourteen-year-old son and I listened. This is what you should be good at if you want to hitchhike. Everybody needs somebody to talk to and people will tell a stranger things they'd never tell their own spouse. They know they'll never see you again and they know you'll never meet the people in their story either, so they feel free to go ahead and tell the truth.

John said he doesn't know where his son gets it. Kid is a straight-A student, always has been. And he's playing on the high school basketball team even though he's still in junior high.

"Boy's just got the fire in him."

He talked about his son until he'd covered everything that amazed him about this child of his, then talked about his daughter.

"Damned if she ain't a straight-A girl herself. And she's gonna need 'em if she wants to get into that school."

His daughter wanted to go to the Air Force Academy in Colorado Springs.

"And I'll bet she will. I'll just bet she will."

John dropped me off where the road splits. It was a desolate place. At the three-way there was a wooden cross in the weeds: *Tara Swanson—Nov 20, 1973, May 24, 1998—Tara We Miss You.* If you're looking, you can find memorials like this on practically every curve on every highway in America.

It was still snowing, but only lightly. A rancher in a tractor was hauling hay out to a herd of cattle. Some 1950s automobiles were sinking into the snowdrifts. I paced back and forth to keep warm. I hung around the intersection, but I didn't sit down. Sitting makes you look lazy. Americans don't like lazy. Americans in their cars believe they deserve to be there because they've worked hard for it, and if you can't even get up on your feet, you don't deserve a ride.

Three big automobiles passed by in a row. Each was loaded with older women. Must have been a club of some kind. Cow Belles, a church group. They were obviously full so I just waved. Some of the women frowned at me disapprovingly; some waved back; some looked away as if I were roadkill.

Twenty minutes went by before another vehicle appeared. It was a semi, rolling steady as a steam engine through the storm. Truckers don't stop for hitchhikers anymore. Their insurance forbids it. I'd decided not even to stick out my thumb, then abruptly did it anyway.

Next thing I knew I heard the whoosh of the brakes, the engine groaning, the tranny downshifting, and the tractor-trailer shuddered to a stop—dead in the middle of the road. The door swung open above my head and I climbed up into the cab.

"Been standing there long?" The driver had a good-natured, saggy-jowled, cocker-spaniel face.

"Not too."

I watched him work through the gears, getting the beast back up to speed.

"Eighteen of 'em," he said. "Some trucks have ten, some fourteen. Eighteen's better if you're running a lot of up and down."

He was wearing a trucker's baseball cap, had forearms thick as thighs, and a vast belly. I thought he must have been a trucker his whole life.

"Nope. Started four years ago."

He said he's doing it for the money.

"Wife is getting used to it now. Learning how to do a few things 'round the house that I used to do. My boys are fifteen and twenty and pretty much doing their own thing. They don't miss me that much."

He's only home two nights a week. Rest of the nights he sleeps in his cab. He eats in his cab too, cooking off a hot plate to save a little money. He doesn't like the truckstops and only uses them for a shower.

"Ten hours or 600 miles every day." He doesn't doctor his books.

"I guess you could say I live here, right in here, all the time. They told me when I first started that being a trucker was a lifestyle, not a job. They turned out to be right about that at least."

"What do you do at night?"

"Read. I got a little TV but I like reading better." He threw his eyes back over his shoulder toward a stack of paperbacks on his bunk.

He talked about his sons as we cruised through Cowdrey and Walden, and then traversed the hay fields of North Park, riding far above the ground blizzards writhing across the road. He dropped me off at Muddy Pass. He was continuing west on Highway 40 to Craig, to deliver a load of hay.

"Was good to have your company, but just so nothing gets back to anybody, I'd appreciate it if you didn't remember me."

Muddy Pass is down the road from Rabbit Ears Pass, which is above Steamboat Springs. People in SUVs with the latest skis clamped in the latest ski racks blasted past me. I didn't care. Three good rides and I was on a roll.

It was snowing hard now, soaking my jeans. I half-wished I hadn't shaved, but facial hair is out. So is long hair. Leather jackets. Ragged anything. All our mothers told us not to judge a book by its cover, and every one of us does it all the time. You want a ride, you need to look normal. Like somebody's brother just trying to get home from college.

If you look strange, strange people will pick you up. Strange people are supposed to be interesting, but usually they're just messed up, and if you happen to get caught up even for fifteen minutes in their messed-up lives, you can get killed. They'll be drinking or doing dope and driving ninety-five and want you to be cool like they are and if you won't they get their feelings hurt and then start scheming in their paranoid heads and pretty soon one of them will try grabbing your throat from behind and everything will go haywire and they'll roll the car.

But it's not only looks. Posture is also important. No slouching. Shoulders back, chin up, both hands out of your pockets. Have your hands hidden in your pockets and people don't know if you have something in them or not and they'll start imagining all kinds of things. Stand natural, not trying to conceal anything about yourself, looking like all you want is a ride, because that's the truth. Your hitching arm should be slightly bent, steady but relaxed. Never stretch your arm out and lean into the traffic or jug your arm up and down. That makes you look desperate. Desperation's one of those things people will go clear out of their way to avoid.

After a while, a little car stopped and I folded myself clumsily into the back seat. Reggae music, chimes hanging from the mirror, peace sticker on the window.

"I'm Emily," said the driver.

"I'm Justin," said the young man in the passenger seat.

They both reached back between the seats to vigorously shake my hand. They were on their way to an Earth First! meeting in Boulder. They were so happy to see me I might as well have been family.

Emily had just finished studying in India for two years, was spending three months with her family down in a remote part of Mexico this spring, and would be going to Colorado College in the fall. Justin had camped out, hanging high up in trees in Oregon to protest clear-cutting and was bound for Chile to study permaculture. They were planning to save the world. I found myself envious—I was once like them. They gave me hope.

"Earth First!" Justin expounded, "is a nonorganization made up of nonmembers dedicated to not giving up."

When they dropped me off in Dillon, Justin tore a strip from a poetry paperback and wrote down his e-mail address. As they drove away, I turned the scrap over in my hand to find the last line of a poem: "You shall above all things be glad and young."

I shouldered the pack and walked to the I-70 on-ramp. It wasn't a big pack. People see a big pack and they have an excuse: I don't have room. On the other hand, hitchhiking without a pack is worse. People wonder what you're doing out there with nothing. They're thinking and they're probably right that anybody who's legitimate is carrying a pack. If he doesn't have a pack then he probably isn't going anywhere. If he isn't going anywhere then why's he got his thumb out wanting you to pull over and let him inside your car.

I've seen a few people hitching with a suitcase, but that's weird. People with suitcases are the kind of people who should be taking a bus or the train, or someone who's hoping someone will listen to them for a while and then talk them out of it and drive them back home.

A pickup pulled over.

"Just throw it in the back."

I slung the pack in the empty bed of the pickup.

Guy's name was Bobby. "I hitched myself for fifteen months," he said.

I wondered why he was so specific.

"DUI. Lost my driver's license. But everything works out for the best. I learned a lot about people, having to hitchhike every day."

Bobby said he gave his life to Jesus about a year ago and hasn't touched alcohol since. He went ten miles out of his way to drop me off on Highway 91.

I was standing beside a snowdrift when a husky came trotting up to me and nuzzled my hand. No fear of strangers whatsoever. I scrubbed his lower back and his tail went mad, then he traveled on, content as only dogs know how to be.

I've met people hitching with a dog, but it's dumb. Dog people like dogs, but the rest of the world is full of cat people or people ambivalent to the animal kingdom. I've also met people hitching with other kinds of pets, mostly small animals they hide inside their coats. They feel out the situation to see whether they should show the driver their friend. I've met people with gerbils and snakes and guinea pigs and ferrets.

A corollary to no pets is no pals. Two guys standing on the road looks too much like two guys either trying to get away from trouble or trying to get into it.

I was standing there pondering this when the driver of a car going maybe sixty slammed on the brakes and fishtailed to a stop.

I looked through the window before opening the car door. The driver was staring straight ahead, both hands on the steering wheel. He had a crew cut, a scar on his forehead, and a tattoo of a cross on his left hand. He was wearing Carhartt overalls splattered with cement mud. The car was a mess inside. I got in.

The first few minutes in a car with a stranger are always the most tense. You've got all your antennae working to figure out the score, and so does the driver. You can both feel the vibes. It's as if every human is surrounded by their own electromagnetic field. Most of the time a simple conversation starts itself and the atmosphere soon clears, but not always.

I once got into a Cadillac in Iowa. The car was immaculate inside and out. So was the driver, even though he was probably ninety years old. He didn't say a word for half an hour. He just drove smoothly through the cornfields. He eventually turned his white head toward me and said, "Well, if you're plannin' on killin' me, you might as well git it over with." I didn't know whether to laugh or cry. After I finally convinced him that I didn't want anything more than a lift, he told me how he'd fought in the Great War and then hitchhiked from New York City back to Iowa. "I was still in uniform," he said. "There weren't many cars but not one ever passed me by." He ended up taking me to the VFW and forcing me to eat two whole meals because he said I looked like I could use a little meat on my bones.

Now I introduced myself to the driver.

"Calvin," he said, and we shook. His hand was thick with muscle.

I took a guess. "You lay concrete."

"Sewer line."

I got him to tell me a little about his work, but he wasn't the talkative kind so I left it alone. He drove fast but knew how. At one gas station he bought us both candy bars, at the next I bought us plastic-encased burritos.

Calvin was going home to Antonito to see his girlfriend and visit his family. After a few hours, as we got closer, he began to modestly point out the roadside attractions. A crocodile farm. The Jack Dempsey museum. A UFO observatory.

It was dusk when we pulled into Antonito. It had been the best ride of the day. Long, fast, no small talk. He showed me a house-cum-castle built of aluminum cans, then dropped me off.

Highway 285 south into New Mexico is a lonesome stretch, especially at night. The only vehicle that passed me was a Colorado State

Patrol car. I didn't have my thumb out, but the patrolman knew exactly what I was up to. He also knew that I knew that if I was still here when he passed by again, he'd pick me up.

Hitchhiking is against the law almost everywhere. But the law is as malleable as the people who enforce it. I must have been picked up by the highway patrol fifty times. They put you in the backseat and run a check on you to make sure you didn't kill anybody lately. Then you get the lecture about how hitchhiking is illegal and they could put you in jail just like that if they wanted to. Be polite and keep your lip zipped and they'll sometimes just let you out and tell you to disappear.

The moon was up when the cop came back. A tractor-trailer was lumbering by and I had my thumb out. I was less than a hundred miles from Santa Fe, but nobody stops when it's dark. For one thing they can't see you until their headlights hit you, and then you can't help but look like a ghost or a prison escapee.

The cop was turning around and I was wondering if I might not be spending the night in the Conejos County jail when the eighteen-wheeler inexplicably roared to a halt and the cab door uncorked like an opening in the night sky.

We made it to Santa Fe in two hours, riding through the velvet desert counting shooting stars.

The Bear

The water is so low the stumps cast long, inescapable shadows across the swamp. The stumps are jagged and barkless, as if this were once a battlefield. Then the battle moved on, leaving these rigid, truncated bodies propped up in the water.

Greg and I paddle in unison, gliding the canoe, matched in motivation and intent. Having seen it all before, Greg sits in the stern, broad and big-shouldered, deftly wielding a hand-hewn paddle. I kneel in the bow like a youth on his first hunt, my paddle small and light. We pull ourselves past the massive cypress stumps. Some are thirty feet in circumference, bulged out at the base as if a bomb had gone off inside. Most rise twelve feet above the surface of the swamp, then stop, vanish, whatever they once were gone forever.

Dangling by a cord from a limb is a half-submerged cage. We come alongside and Greg pulls up the trap. It's a handmade crawfish catcher—a large tube fashioned from chicken wire. It's empty.

"Settin' on the ground," Greg says. "Can't catch a thing that way. That's how low the water is in the basin. Crawfish might not even run this year."

Greg Guirard is a part-time crawfisherman—but then he's a Cajun, so he's a part-time everything: logger, writer, photographer, philosopher. He grew up on the West Atchafalaya Levee, between the hamlets of Catahoula and Henderson, poling a pirogue in the Atchafalaya Basin, hunting whitetail, catching catfish. His father once owned a lumber mill along the levee canal. Greg has spent almost all of his sixty-three years in the swamp. Several times he tried to leave—for Belize, for Costa Rica, for Virginia—but the swamp called him back.

Greg drops the trap.

"'Nother couple years like this and I don't know what'll happen. I don't want to even say what'll happen."

He takes up his paddle and puts his solid body into the stroke. The bow of the canoe bounces and we go on across the water through the forest of stumps.

For many years Greg taught English at Louisiana State University in Lafayette. Back then he was married and had four children, and he raised cattle on the levee and ran crawfish traps, but even with teaching it wasn't enough. He loved literature and loved teaching it, but he left the university in 1973 after he found himself $30,000 in debt. A few years later he went back to making a living from the swamp.

One of his students had given him a camera, and he began taking pictures when he was out working on the water. The camera was like a fishing rod: you never knew quite what you were going to get. Sometimes you just brought it along on a whim and caught something you would never have imagined. Other times you went out and worked at it all day and still came home empty-handed. Greg took pictures of the moss-draped trees and the stilt-legged birds and the hazel water, of hunters with their dogs and fishermen with their nets, of raccoon pelts nailed to barns. And he took pictures of stumps. In 1983 he completed the first of four self-published books, *Seasons of Light in the Atchafalaya Basin*, in which his photographs are accompanied by two famous stories by William Faulkner. Faulker is his favorite author.

"He wrote all kinds of different stories," said Greg. "Came about as close as a human can come to the truth."

Sometimes it seems as though every story is a circumfluent, involuted Faulkner story; we just lack the burning craft to tell it like he did.

In 1985 Greg's first book was given as a Christmas gift to a close friend of mine. Although living in Chicago, he was originally from

Mississippi, where as a boy reading mountaineering books he had yearned for a life in the mythic West. He obtained this life when he moved from Chicago to Wyoming, where we met, and fell into an ever-deepening conversation about literature and life. One day he lent me Greg's book and it birthed in me a yearning to go to the mythic bayou. Being one who believes every day might be my last, I dialed directory assistance for Catahoula, Louisiana, and got Greg Guirard's phone number. I got around to my question after we talked through photography and Faulkner and fishing.

"So, has anyone ever paddled across the Atchafalaya?"

"You mean 'cross the whole thing? One side to the other, levee to levee?"

"I guess."

"Not in my lifetime, far's I know. Everybody has a motorboat. They only use the pee-rogue to check nets in the thick places."

But he'd said he'd ask around and call me back.

A few days later the phone rang.

"Nobody," he said. "Maybe not for almost a hundred years. Little two-horse outboard motor came to the bayou way back, around 1910, and that was that."

"You want to do it?"

Greg didn't know me from Adam. I was a Northerner's voice on the phone.

"You ever been down here?"

"Nope."

"You ever pee-rogued?"

"Nope."

"Canoe works better. I'll cook up some jambalaya."

I stopped at the end of a tunnel of dark down a dirt road. There was still a light on at the house hidden in the trees, but it was two A.M. I was planning to just sleep in the car when suddenly there was a hulking figure coming toward me. I got out of the car.

"Made it," he said.

My hand disappeared into his.

"Good directions," I said.

We sat at the kitchen table in his house deep in the woods that was just a ramshackle hunting camp on the edge of the swamp when his family moved here and wasn't so much more now. To get to school Greg and his brother had had to paddle three miles down the canal to Catahoula. They only spoke French—or rather, Cajun French—just like the other waterborn waterbred Cajun kids, all of them like some endangered and disappearing swamp species that hasn't yet acquired webbed feet or gills. First Greg's brother and later his own children left the swamp behind and moved to big cities. Greg and his wife divorced in 1989, and he only recently remarried. His second wife, Kathy Martin, is a blues singer and Tarot card reader from N'Orleans who learned how to read cards from a six-foot-five blond Bourbon Street transvestite named Morgana.

Greg spread out the maps of the Atchafalaya, pushing aside an alligator skull and several slices of fungus-eaten cypress used as hot pads for all that burning bayou cuisine which he had already told me any self-respecting Cajun male made himself, and carefully penciled our route across the swamp.

"Figure it'll take two and a half, three days."

We went to bed after three, got up at five, loaded his loaded aluminum canoe into the bed of his pickup, drove down the levee, and slipped into Bayou Benoit before dawn.

I had ignorantly imagined the Louisiana swamp as muggy, buggy, and hot. But on this particular morning the water was cold and black and the air was chilly and the bugs apparently too stiff to fly. We paddled hard down Grand Bayou into Lake Fausse Point Cut, partly to push some miles beneath the bow before the sun came up, partly to stay warm. The skin of the water was rough. Only when the sky started opening up did the water change, smoothing out and harmonizing in blue hues.

"This is the magic time," said Greg.

But the words were hardly out of his mouth before we disappeared into the Texaco Location Canal. It was overgrown and unused, like hundreds of other canals dredged through the Atchafalaya like a hatchwork of highways after oil was discovered in the 1930s. Huge platforms were built throughout the basin to support the machines that pumped out the crude until it was almost gone. Then the big companies started selling off their fields to contractors who squeezed out the last of the oil and were supposed to cap the wells and remove the platforms, but didn't. We would pass a dozen oil platforms, most rotting and abandoned, but Greg would hardly seem to notice them, as though they had been here so long they belonged in the swamp.

We broke back out into sunlight on Jackass Bay. Here were the giant stumps with their long shadows and occasionally a forlorn crawfish trap shipwrecked on protruding cypress knees. After checking another cage Greg pointed with his paddle to a dry waterline eight feet up one of the stumps.

"That's how high the water was once," he told me, "but they won't let it in here anymore. Half the crawfishermen already got out. Even Roy Blanchard. He used to be the best in the basin. Now he works as a janitor for a hotel on Highway 10."

The entire Atchafalaya Basin is a neglected spillway for the Mississippi River. The nation's largest waterway comes wriggling down from the north, turns left at the corner of Mississippi and Louisiana, diagonals southeast through Baton Rouge and New Orleans, and lolls on out a delta shaped like the head of an alligator. But rivers, not unlike humans, like to take the line of least resistance, and the Mississippi knows this circuitous course is not the fastest way to the sea. For hundreds of years it has been leaking more and more of itself into the Atchafalaya Basin, and it would probably have taken the shortcut decades ago—veering right rather than left just north of Baton Rouge, breaching the silt bars, pouring full-bodied into the Atchafalaya distributary, and rushing straight down to the beach—if the Army Corps of Engineers hadn't stepped in.

"The Mississippi was too important to be captured," said Greg. "What would happen to Union Carbide, Dow Chemical, Georgia-Pacific?"

These companies all needed the Mississippi to barge their bulky products from New Orleans to ports the world over. First the Corps built levees, and then more levees—wherever the Mississippi was threatening to spill due south. But the basin was still needed as an overflow valve, so locks were put in.

"In flood years they open the gates and fresh water flushes through the basin and the crawfish flourish and the fishermen make a living," said Greg. "In low-water years most of the water is kept in the Mississippi to float the industrial boats.

"But it might change," he added. "Might just get better."

Greg and other environmentalists and defenders of the Cajun way of life have been negotiating with the Corps of Engineers for decades. Still, his optimism seemed odd to me. I was beginning to understand that that's the kind of man he was. He looked for, and perhaps even saw, the good in people and places and possibility.

Beyond Jackass Bay we slid up into the Range Line Cut, a narrow, almost subterranean canal. You would think that in a swamp the water would all be flat, almost by definition, but conflicting green water was gushing down against us.

"Just never know!" exclaimed Greg joyfully.

We put our backs into the paddles and pumped our arms and the canoe bobbed up and down. I was bent out over the prow, digging hard, concentrating, when Greg shouted, "You ever seen that movie *African Queen?*" I glanced over my shoulder and he nodded toward the bank and I saw it was moving the wrong way.

We both stepped out of the boat and sank up to our waists in cold, rushing water that knocked us backward. We grabbed the canoe and struggled up onto the bank, thinking it might be easier to line the boat along, but it wasn't. Everywhere the bank was either impossibly slick with mud or impossibly overgrown. We slid back into the swirling canal and began plowing upstream, thrashing and slipping, me pulling, Greg pushing, water snakes curling around our bellies and razor-toothed garfish shooting between our legs. Without a boat, humans are as fit for water as turtles without legs. Still, we eventually reached a tiny logjam, portaged up and over, and shoved off onto another expanse of flat water and giant stumps.

"Now," said Greg. "Now we're in the middle of the middle of the Atchafalaya. This is the Red-Eye Swamp. Named for the primeval glint in an alligator's eyes."

As if to reward us for having gotten ourselves here by dint of our own stubborn sinew, birds began sweeping in around us. They keeled between the stumps in the still air, planing just above the water while Greg called out to them by name.

"Kingfisher. Anhinga. Turkey buzzard. Tree sparrow."

I spotted something orange.

"Cardinal!" His voice was high. I suddenly realized that the idea of crossing the swamp had been a pretext. Although it was something he could tell his grandkids about, paddling across the swamp really meant paddling into it, penetrating that one place on the planet he held in his heart as a refuge.

"Snowy egret. Wood duck. Coot. Look at 'em all!"

I was watching the birds and all the hope they seemed to carry so lightly, and yet they were still weaving through stumps—sad, monstrous monuments to human greed.

Before the Army Corps of Engineers shut off the natural spigot and the swamp started silting in and the crawfish started dying, before the oil barons chopped up the swamp and sucked out all the oil and then left, there were the lumber barons. The Atchafalaya was once like the redwood forests. There were a million acres of ancient cypress, and loggers came from all over the country to cut it down. Everybody believed it would last forever. Every fence, water tank, barge, bunk house, and sugar mill in Louisiana was built with old-growth cypress, some planks measuring six feet across. Commercial logging started just after the Civil War and the last cypress was hacked down in 1930. Every solitary tree, apart from those that were hollow or diseased, was taken—the entire Atchafalaya Basin, levee-to-levee, clear-cut.

Paddling onward, Greg was still naming birds—"Prothonotary warbler. Pileated woodpecker. Barred owl"—as if we were actually in a forest. As if in his mind he could still see the majestic cypress rising from the swamp, as if he could still see the world wild and rich and vulnerable the way it was before he was born. It seemed naive. This was the ghost of a forest.

After we passed out of the open water he was silent for some time before telling me that he once wrote a novel.

"But it didn't sell," he said. "The photography books sell. People like pictures because they're pretty, not because they tell the truth."

"What was the title of your novel?"

"*The Land of Dead Giants*."

It didn't take us three days to canoe across the Atchafalaya Basin. It took eight hours. Greg was surprised. We hadn't paddled fast, only steady, but the swamp is not a big place, on the map if not in the mind. Twenty miles wide, less than a hundred long; even with all our meandering we probably only traveled twenty-five miles. I was some- how saddened that our journey had ended so quickly. It was as though much of the mystery of the Atchafalaya had suddenly been lost. Greg sensed my disappointment.

"So, Mark," Greg said, as we stepped into the water and pulled the canoe up onto the East Levee, "you want to go logging?"

"Logging!"

"Actually, I call it 'resurrecting.'"

The next morning we motored out into the swamp in an aluminum skiff. Deep among the stumps, Greg cut the engine. Dangling by a rope cinched around a limb protruding from a blackened stump, was a half-submerged log.

"Pull it up," Greg said, laughing.

I could barely move it.

When the Atchafalaya was clear-cut, some of the densest logs—so ancient and compressed and full of oil that they wouldn't even float—sank out of sight. Ever since giving up teaching, Greg has been prying these "sinkers" from the mud during the dry season, roping chunks of foam around their bellies, and waiting for high water to set them afloat. He sells the wood to sculptors or custom furniture makers or anybody who just wants a solid piece of what once was.

"It's a way for people to see what we all lost, what the world lost," said Greg. "Cypress is the most beautiful wood in the world."

We wrestled with this one lost-and-found log for half a day before finally pulling it ashore.

On the day I left, Greg told me he had one last place to show me.

Along the levee, on a corner of the land that had been passed down in his family from generation to generation, he had started a forest. He had hand-planted tulip poplar, black nut, swamp chestnut oak, six varieties of red oak—twenty-five species in all—and in the very middle, where the water pooled, 1,500 cypress trees. It's a cool green world of slim-waisted, ten-year-old trees that will one day, someday, be giants.

He had placed a bench among the cypress and we sat there together. On the bench, wrapped in opaque plastic, was a book. It was a book by Faulkner, of course, one that includes a story called "The

Bear"—a tale of "that doomed wilderness whose edges were being constantly and punily gnawed at by men with plows and axes who feared it because it was wilderness, men myriad and nameless even to one another in the land where the old bear had earned a name, and through which ran not even a mortal beast but an anachronism indomitable and invincible out of an old dead time, a phantom, epitome and apotheosis of the old wild life. . . ."

When Greg first read this story, in 1961, he was so moved he had to see this mythic bear for himself, so he drove all the way to the Audubon Zoo in New Orleans.

Greg told me he still reads this story every year, even though he knows, in the end, the bear is killed.

Going to Hell

That only he deserves his life, his freedom,
Who wins them every day anew.
    —Goethe, *Faust*, Part II, Act V, Scene 7

It was raining when I set off through the mountains in a rental Fiat barely bigger than a go-cart. The windows fogged immediately. I swabbed the glass with a sleeve. The road corkscrewed along cliffs and beneath overhangs like all half-paved, one-lane roads in the backlands of Greece. For some reason—hope perhaps, fear, curiosity—I was driven by a sense of urgency. The wheels of the matchbox car were so tiny and treadless that I almost skidded off a misty, hairpin precipice before realizing I shouldn't be in any hurry to get where I was going.

Through the drizzle, I began to notice that at almost every airy turn there was a metal box with a cross welded on top. At first I thought they might be mailboxes for forgotten bentback farmers, but they were too big, too ominous. I finally pulled over to examine one. It was two foot square, once painted blue but now faded almost to white, with a plate glass window. Inside was a candle in a bronze bowl, a box of matches, a bottle of olive oil, a bottle of wine, a framed picture of the bloodied, beatific Jesus, and a black-and-white photo of a man with a drink in his hand, grinning wildly, toasting some unknown occasion.

Back behind the wheel, I slowed down to peer into each shrine I passed by. In a few the candle was burning. Others contained personal effects: a pocketwatch, a necklace, a book. In three hours of mountain driving I passed over thirty reliquaries. Where the road dropped down onto the plain of Acheron, I pulled off beside one of these small monuments to lost life, reached across to the passenger seat, took up my college copy of the Odyssey, and read Circe's words to Odysseus: "You must go to the house of Hades and awful Persephoneia, to ask directions from Teiresias the blind Theban seer."

Travel long and far enough, physically or metaphysically, and you'll eventually lose your bearings. It can't be helped. When it happens, no matter where you are or what you're doing, all you really want is to go home.

It happened to me in Switzerland. I had come to climb the north face of the Matterhorn, but the day I arrived in Zermatt it started snowing, and it dumped nonstop for almost a week. Every morning I went trudging into the mountains hoping against hope, and every night I slunk down to the North Wall Bar, played chess with the local climbers, and did pull-ups on the door frame to win free pints of lager and pans of pizza. Then I'd stumble back to the Bahnhof Hotel and read Homer.

On the sixth day, the day I flew out, it was still snowing. But I didn't fly home. I could have—should have, perhaps—but Homer had gotten to me.

Most people pitch Homer five seconds after taking the final exam. I did. At a certain age, however, you start thinking you might have learned something when you were young if you hadn't already been so smart. I was rereading the Odyssey because it is arguably the world's first novel, the original thriller, composed 700 years before the birth of Christ. It's also the seminal adventure book, chronicling the surreal travels and travails of an alpha adventurer, the hubristic yet humble Odysseus, who sails away from Ithaca to fight the good fight, sneaks into Troy and dismembers his enemies, blinds the Cyclops with a burning pole, has all-night sex with Calypso. But his most daring adventure is to visit Hades. Why did he go there? For answers only the underworld could provide, and for directions home. After years of sailing beyond the edge of the known world, Odysseus had lost his bearings.

Days of unconsummated mountain climbing are not unlike windless days at sea. You eventually grow weary and frustrated and begin to conjure questions that experience cannot answer. On the fifth day of snow in Zermatt I bought a map of Greece. Odysseus got answers when he visited the underworld. I thought the place might be worth a visit.

Homer, like all learned Greeks, freely mixed geography with cosmology. Hence he was quite specific about the location of hell on earth: it could be found at the confluence of the Acheron, "river of pain," the Pyriphlegethon, "blazing with fire," and the Cocytos, "resounding with lamentations, which is a branch of the hateful water of the Styx." Where the three rivers merged there was a great stone, and beneath the stone, a cave—the entrance to the underworld.

I found the Acheron on the map. Almost 3,000 years later and it was still right there, doglegging through the Pindus Mountains just south of the Albanian border.

Odysseus sailed to Hades; I flew. Nonetheless, my journey began as any proper trip to hell should. The plane sat on the tarmac for over an hour, with jet fuel fumes seeping into the cabin until passengers started to faint. There was a heart attack on board somewhere over the Alps and the flight was diverted to Milan. We arrived in Athens a half-day late. I missed my connection north and my rusksack was sent to baggage purgatory—somewhere in Slovakia. I hiked around Athens in the polluted heat for three days before giving up on the bags and flying to Ioannina with just the shirt on my back and enough cash to get a rental car.

In a village where the old men wear black berets, sit at an outdoor café, smoke, play cards, and stare disapprovingly at slow-moving vehicles, I drove up to a half-hidden blue sign with an arrow and the word "Nekromanteio." Turned right, chugged up a steep cobblestone path lined with whitewashed cottages, passed into a sparse wood, and parked behind two European tour buses disembouching crowds of bluehairs and bony-kneed husbands of all nations. I should have known hell would be just one more stop on a package tour.

I paid the entrance fee at the iron gate, bought the color brochure, and began wandering around the ancient ruins and taking snapshots in the rain with all the other camera-clicking idiots. The site itself lies atop a small knoll surrounded by scarred poplars. Fanning out in all directions is the floodplain of the three dark rivers I'd read about. The ruins consist of the shell of an eighteenth-century Greek Orthodox monastery defiantly built right over hell. Beneath the monastery is a labyrinthine passageway that leads to a hole in the stone floor. Below is a crypt—a chamber purported to be the cave that Homer described in the *Odyssey* as the entrance to Hades.

I had circled through the wet ruins and the labyrinth and gotten in line, ready to descend into the mouth of hell, when a nasal Texas drawl screeched up from the hole: "Lemme out. Lemme OUT! It smells down 'n here." Then another voice, blasé and male: "Aw, honey, go ta hell." A roar of cackling.

Suddenly I realized this wasn't right. This wasn't the way to visit Hades, the sacrosanct Land of the Dead—in broad daylight with tour guides wearing too much makeup shouting at their bespectacled sheep. It was heretical. Blasphemous. I turned around and left, noting on the way out that hell closes every day at two-thirty P.M.

I drove back into the village, parked at the café of old men, ordered a bottle of retsina and a plate of yemista, and begin studying the brochure. It was written by an archaeologist and included a lengthy account of Odysseus's visit, as well as photographs and intricate diagrams. I committed the floor plans to memory.

On the second bottle of retsina I remembered the first time someone told me I was going to hell. It was three decades ago in Sunday school class with the medieval Mrs. Teuful. I was having problems with this idea of a merciful God in a world full of suffering. If God was so damn merciful, why didn't he just help us out?

"Young man!" Mrs. Teuful admonished. "You'll go to hell for asking such questions."

Some years later, as should happen to every young man, I was told to go to hell moments before receiving a stinging, Hollywood-worthy slap from a woman. More years later I was told to go to hell by someone who read what I had written about him and believed I should be severely punished.

That's what hell is for most Christians: a netherworld where the wicked get what's coming to them. It hath been such since the time of the Apostles. Saint Peter described hell as a place of "unquenchable fire" where there was a "great gnashing of teeth among the children" and sinners were "hung up by their tongues" or "by their loins" and tormented by worms and venomous beasts. Charles the Fat, King of Swabia in the late 800s, described hell as a place of "inextricable punishments" where infidels suffer in "boiling rivers and liquid metal." The clergy of the dark ages loved this stuff. So did Hieronymus Bosch.

But the Hades of Homer was less vengeful. There were those who were punished—Sisyphus forever shouldering the great stone uphill, Tantalus chin-deep in water and dying of thirst, Tityos with his liver repeatedly torn out by vultures—but most of the inhabitants of Hades were there only because they were dead. For the Greeks, Hades was simply where the soul went when the body expired. And these souls, no longer bound by the shackles of time, had one tremendous gift: they could see into the future. Hades was a realm of oracles. Odysseus went there not only to find his way home, but to discover his destiny.

I returned to the Nekromanteio at dusk. The rain had stopped and a purple shroud hung over the valley. I came up behind the ruins through the darkling trees and encountered a stone wall. I had expected a fence of some kind, but this section of the ruins was set upon a high rampart. Since there was probably a night watchman at the front entrance, my only choice was to scale the wall.

It was near dark as I began climbing. The stones were covered in moss and dripping with phlegmlike liquid. I moved as quickly as possible. Near the top I lost my footing and only by the luck of a desperate lunge managed to clutch a stanchion above my head. Adrenaline poured into my blood as I pulled myself up and surreptitiously flipped over the spiked fence.

I had to feel my way along the broken walls to find the opening to the labyrinth. I could see nothing. With my arms stretched out before me, I glided along the twisting path, as if by coming here at night I had become a phantom myself. I found an iron rail and traced it. I knew I was standing above the crypt when I smelled a dank, almost putrid air exhaling upward from the orifice. My feet found stairs dropping steeply into the subterranean chamber.

At the bottom of the stairs I stopped and stared sightlessly into nothingness. A damp chill touched my face. The stench of wet dirt filled my nostrils. I tried stepping forward but the ground was slick, as if still wet with the blood of ancient sacrifice.

When Odysseus was here he saw the ghost of his mother and spoke with her. He met the fathers of his fellow warriors and told them of their sons' great deeds in battle. He even spoke to Achilles, his friend who had fallen in battle.

I waited in blackness. It had all seemed like a lark, really, until this moment. Then something strange began. A primeval desire welled up inside me, and as I stood blind and silent above the bowels of the earth I realized I actually did want what Odysseus had wanted: answers. I wished with all my heart for those I'd lost to return, to speak with me, to share their cosmic secrets, for the light of their faces to illuminate this inky pit. But no one came to see me. Not the too many dead friends and lovers with whom I'd drunk and slept and struggled and whom I could not save from falling in the wars of life; nor my dead relatives, men and women who carried me upon their shoulders or in their hearts or in their stories. I strained with my eyes wide open in hopes of making out kith or kin in the impenetrable, eternal midnight . . . but nothing.

I don't know how long I waited in darkness, but no mysteries were revealed to me. Odysseus was more fortunate. His mother told him that his wife, Penelope, was still faithful and that his son, Telemachos, had become a brave prince. Teiresias instructed him in how to find and fight his way back home, and assured him that he would complete his journey and live a long, contented life. "Death ever so peaceful shall take you off when comfortable old age shall be your only burden," said the blind seer, "and your people shall be happy 'round you."

Odysseus was the luckiest of great travelers, perhaps because he was also the most courageous, but more likely because he believed. He had faith. For me, one of the multitudinous modern-day agnostics, it would be asking too much to be given answers to the mysteries of life. The faithless are forever searching.

I retraced my steps back up out of the crypt, back through the labyrinth, and out into the night of ruins in the valley of the Styx.

If going to hell was easier than I had expected—which is what I should have expected—getting out turned into a nightmare.

Some days later I dropped off the rental car in Ioannina to fly back to Athens. The plane, of course, was late. One hour, two hours, four. Eventually a woman behind the ticket counter announced that the plane was not coming. The waiting room exploded. Greek men with bellies hanging over their pants began bellowing, women in black high heels began screaming, little children started crying.

In the pandemonium I bumped into a Canadian surgical supplies salesman named Terry and his Greek partner, Marina. They specialized in replacement parts for human hearts. Bereft of an airlift, Terry and Marina had decided to hire a taxi and drive the length of Greece in one night. Why not?

It was raining again, but the taxi was a Mercedes and the driver inexplicably cautious. We ate at a roadside café at one in the morning and pushed on to the Gulf of Patras, where we changed taxis and drivers and took a ferry across the dark waters to the Peloponnesian peninsula. As soon as we docked, the taxi shot out of the ferry like a bat out of hell. The new driver had demonic eyes, a torturer's smile, and a death wish. The road was slick as black ice and he loved it. Curves posted at ninety kilometers per hour he took at no less than 140. I kept involuntarily grabbing the dashboard. At one point, in desperation, I glanced up at his license strapped to the visor, but the photo was a chiaroscuro blur, and the letters of his named smudged. C-H-A-R-O-something.

Back on a straightaway, he gunned the engine and my eyes dropped down to the speedometer. We were going 200 kph, so fast that the rain flew straight over the windshield without even getting it wet. As we went flying around the next black bend, starting to hydroplane—seemingly about to smash through the guardrail, sail off the cliff, and be dashed upon the jagged rocks stabbing up out of the ocean—the headlights caught, for the briefest possible moment, the ghostly image of a dripping metal box with a cross on top and a dim, guttering candle within.

The Bike Messenger

Oct. 29, Lhasa—Back from the mountain. Another failed expedition. Two months of cold and struggle and unfulfilled dreams. Nothing worked out as expected. I no longer know why I am here.

Everyone else had already left. I remember I was so restless I couldn't sleep. I rose very early every morning, slipped into the street, and walked past the orphan girl asleep under the cardboard, her face pressed against the cobblestone.

I walked the squalid backstreets of Lhasa until nine o'clock when I could rent a bicycle. Thereafter I rode. I went to lunch at a café run by a New Zealand girl who washed up in Tibet after a year-long pilgrimage. I brought along aeronautical charts and studied the mountains north of the Himalayas while I ate.

One morning I got up, packed silently, stepped around the orphan girl in the dark, and caught a bus north. It was illegal for me to be on this bus but the Chinese police weren't up yet and the bus driver could care less.

It was so cold all the Tibetans were almost invisible inside their sheepskin coats. Wreaths of white breath filled the bus. We all waited for the sun. The bus traveled at no more than thirty miles an hour and somehow it seemed that if only the bus could go faster, the sun would rise sooner. When sunshine finally gushed through the dust-velveted windows the Tibetans poked their heads from their coats like turtles and started talking to one another.

After nine hours we were on the edge of nowhere and I signaled the bus driver to stop. Hunched inside multiple coats, cloaked in clouds of cigarette smoke, he shrugged his shoulders and lifted his foot off the pedal. The engine stopped bawling and the bus slowed to a quiet stop. I got out, climbed up onto the roof, threw off my pack, and jumped down. The Tibetans stared through the opaque windows. I could see their eyes. They didn't wave. The bus pulled away, gradually disappearing like a boat heading back out to sea.

I was alone. The road, a frail gravel line, disappeared on the horizon in both directions. Soaring white mountains to the left, distant white spikes to the right, a vast corridor of brown tundra down the middle. I sat down on my pack in the middle of the road.

Nov. 3, central Tibet—Thought I'd know where to get off the bus, but didn't. Finally just got off. Expected the map to help but it didn't.

I swung on my pack and began walking back along the road. After a few miles I cut off into the grassland toward a geometrical splotch of brown. As I drew near, dusty children in rags began to appear out of nowhere as if they'd sprouted from the dirt. This happens often in remote places. You are seldom alone no matter how far away you think you are. The children started singing. They grabbed my hands with their cold, callused fingers and we walked into the huddle of mud huts. Adults stooped out from the low doorways and began asking questions. I used a dictionary.

I wanted to rent a pack animal and walk into those mountains—I pointed. They laughed. I said the words for yak, horse, donkey, mule. *Yak? Da? Pung-gu? Thray?* The children howled with delight. After some confusion I realized that there were no beasts of burden in this village. It was too poor. A man with a cigarette dangling from his lower lip led me around the back of his sod shack and showed me my alternative: a bicycle.

I should have known. Tibetans are cowboys. They herd yaks and sheep. A bicycle is the poor cowboy's pony. Never needs to be fed, watered, tethered, sheltered. Won't run away. Won't die in a summer snowstorm. With a pump, a patch kit, and wire, the black metal beast is practically indestructible.

The cowboy's bicycle had no brakes and two flat tires. I tried to rent it for a period of one week, but he refused. He needed it. I could hire it for the day, that was all. And the bike came with its rider. He wanted a few yuan. I gave it to him and he began pumping up the tires while his wife, suckling one child and wiping the green snot from the face of another with her sleeve, made us yak butter tea. Neither tire would take air. They needed patching. This took a long time. I tried to help but it was his bicycle and he wanted to do it. I put up my tent.

Nov. 4, central Tibet—Expected to find a pony. Instead found a man with a black Chinese bike.

In the morning he lashed my pack to the rear rack with leather straps, swung into the saddle, and pedaled off without a word.

We moved across the tundra together. He rode and I ran, then we switched places. The bike slammed through boulder fields without so much as dinging the steel rims. We pushed it through swirling gray streams and brilliant snowbanks. Just after dusk we reached a village at the mouth of a valley that sliced into the white-crowned mountains. As we entered a sod-walled compound, people came rushing toward him. They were relatives of his. He introduced me while dropping the pack off the bike. Both tires were flat. He led his bike in a half-circle as if it were a trained pony, leapt on, and galloped off, disappearing into the darkness.

I set up my tent inside the compound while the Tibetans, curious and silent as ever, looked on. They were all wearing massive sheepskin coats, their hands pulled up inside the long sleeves. Later we drank tea inside their smoky one-room home. They stacked paddies of yak dung on the fire. Once it grew warm enough in the room, they removed their winter coats. They were all thin as skinned coyotes. After a while I couldn't take the smoke anymore and retired to the outdoors.

10 pm—Didn't expect it to be so cold. Thermometer reads 7 degrees. Hands too froze up to write.

When I awoke it was still half-dark. Children were already hauling ice-chunked water and milking yaks, their bare toes showing
through their green Chinese sneakers. I managed to rent another
metal steed, this time for three days, sans rider. The tires were almost
flat but there was no pump. I pedaled into the mountains.

For some reason there was a wide, rutted path running up the
valley. I couldn't understand why until I wheeled around a cliff and
saw the monastery. Whitewashed stone walls, rust-colored turrets,
popping red flags—a castle in the arctic desert. Maroon-robed monks
were coming toward me. I was escorted immediately to the chambers
of the lama. He was seated on a high bed swaddled in extremely
soiled maroon robes. He had a large head and the smell of his body
suffused the low-ceilinged room. He appraised me without speaking
and examined every page of my passport. Then he called in a young
acolyte, his interpreter.

The lama said I was in sacred country and did not have the proper
papers. I said I wanted only to ride my bike into the mountains. The
lama asked why. I said, To be in the mountains, nothing more. He
scrutinized my face. That is all? he asked. I nodded. He smiled for the
first time, clapped his hands, and we were served rancid yak butter
tea. I was ordered to camp inside the monastery walls, but allowed to
carry on the next morning.

I continued bicycling up the valley. I rode all day. On both sides,
black rock walls rose and rose until eventually turning into fearsome
ice ridges. It was hard to keep my balance riding over river stones. I
was riding no faster than one could walk. I saw small herds of black
sheep and gold-colored yaks and shepherd boys and women carrying
bundles of wood. When it grew too dark to keep from crashing, I
stopped and set up camp. I cooked inside the tent by candlelight.

*Nov. 7, somewhere in Tibet—Expected a wilderness. Instead, am riding through an
empty landscape of people. The mountains are incidental.*

When I crawled out of the tent in the morning there was a

woman standing at some distance. She was wearing a heavy black wool dress. There was no sound. During the night the creek had frozen straight down to the ground. I fired up the stove and made myself breakfast in the sun. Holding up a steaming bowl of cereal, I tried calling her over but she didn't move.

I decided to hike for the day. Get a view. I took a bag of nuts and water and marched up a long ridge. The distance was further than I thought but I climbed faster than I expected. For a while I entertained hopes of actually summiting. I thought, Wouldn't that be ironic. But up high the snow became too deep. I would have to cross a col with buried crevasses. For a moment I wished I'd had a partner, but then thought better.

I returned to camp just before dusk and the woman reappeared and stood at a distance. I was tired. I sat down and waited. The sky was orange now and the cold was coming. Eventually she approached.

I don't know how old she was. Her pleated face was the color of sienna, her cheekbones protruding like knobs of stone. Three shiny black braids shot down her back, the ends bound together with red yarn. Over her black wool dress she wore a filthy sheepskin coat that dragged in the dirt.

She sat down beside me and took my hand in hers and began to weep. Her body shook as she cried. After a while she wiped the tears from her cheeks with the back of her hand, smiled weakly, and pulled a small branch of juniper from inside her coat. She put the branch in my hand, then stood up and walked away, down the riverbed in the dark.

I cooked dinner, talked to myself, wrote down exactly what had happened before my hand grew too rigid to hold the pen.

In the morning I packed up and left. As I was pushing the bicycle onto the track the woman appeared again. I rested the bicycle against a rock. She hobbled up to me and pressed a ten-yuan note into my hand. I tried not to take it. In her world of poverty ten yuan was a hundred dollars, five hundred dollars. But she forced it into my palm and closed my hand with her rough fingers. Then she started speaking to me. I tried using the dictionary but it was no use, her speech was too rapid and excited. After she had said everything she had to say she began to open the pack on the bike. I realized she was looking for the juniper. I had it in my pocket. I pulled it out to show her and she nodded and walked away.

Riding down out of the mountains I tried to make sense of it, naturally. Why she had given me money? Why she had given me the juniper branch? Every once in a while, when the path was not too rough and I could ride with one hand, I slipped my hand into my pocket, rubbed the juniper, and then held my fingers to my nose. It was a good smell. It reminded me of the smell of sagebrush when I used to canter my bicycle across the prairie as a boy.

When I rode back by the monastery I was again surrounded by a group of stick-thin young monks in maroon robes. Now we were friends. Once again I met the lama. He wanted to know if I had medicine. I was shown a woman with a lump on her back the size of an apple, a child with a cleft palate, a baby who would not eat. I gave him all I had—one small bottle of ibuprofen.

That night I returned the bicycle to the sod home where I had rented it. I had hoped to ride it out to the road, but they needed it. I camped and started walking in the morning. It took a day. When I got to the road I expected to catch a bus heading back to Lhasa. There was none. I hitched. I caught a ride from a truck that hauled stones and I bounced hard in the empty bed in the frigid wind.

The first stars were coming out. There are so many stars in Tibet, more than any place on earth. At midnight the sky looked like the inside of a jewelry box.

Nov. 11, Lhasa—Back again. Thought I would be ready to go home. Almost.

I rented the same bicycle, the only one with brakes, and rode around the outskirts of the city visiting the monasteries. They were cleaner than the one deep in the mountains. The monks were cleaner and better fed. They courted the tourists. I went further afield, as usual.

One morning I was outside a small monastery before dawn when a group of hinterland Tibetans arrived. They were clearly on their pilgrimage. They were so tattered they may have walked a thousand miles. They were so befouled their hands and faces were black. They looked utterly wild and invincible. They began pulling juniper branches from their sheepskin coats and hurling them into the white hearths at the entrance of the monastery. After prostrating themselves three times they passed inside. I followed them. They moved clockwise through the labyrinthine chambers, fingering their rosaries in the dim candlelight, chanting, prostrating themselves before certain Buddha icons, then leaving money in the placid, stone palms.

They set up their tents a quarter-mile away along a river beside the tents of the other pilgrims.

I found a monk who spoke English. He'd learned it from the tourists in town. He said they gave him more money now that he spoke English. I told him about the woman I had met in the mountains. I wrote down exactly what he said:

Nov. 13, beyond Lhasa—The juniper and the money are offerings to facilitate prayers. Perhaps a child is dying. Perhaps a mother is sick. Perhaps a village is starving. You cannot know. They are not your prayers. You were only the messenger.

The next day I spent six hours pedaling out to a remote, forlorn monastery and offered up the juniper branch to the flames. But I am not a Buddhist. I gave the ten-yuan note to the orphan girl. She is perhaps seven. She is still sleeping every night under a scrap of cardboard in the street, huddling with the scab-covered dogs to stay warm.

Crossing to Safety

We think we're at the end. We think we've done it. The adventure's over, nothing left but crossing one last little creek. We come thrashing through the forest. Our skis, once wings for our feet, protrude from our packs and snag on every branch. Our feet—once dry and wholesome, now taped and torn and bloody—punch insensibly through the last snowdrifts. We can smell the barn.

We're sliding around an icy outcrop, catching ourselves with ski poles, when we first hear it. We stop. Listen.

"It's raging," Ken says calmly.

As we draw near, dropping from pines into aspen, the roar floods up through the trees. We squeeze into the willows and poke our heads out.

The river is brown, sinewy, convulsing like electrically stimulated muscle. It has boiled out of its banks. Chest-deep along the edges, deeper out in the middle, churning with noise. I toss a stick into the prodigal creek and it is sucked out of sight.

We were warned. A week ago we telephoned a rancher up here. "Jakey's Fork is runnin' higher'n a horse. Ain't no gettin' over it." We took this under advisement, then went anyway. We figured we'd cross that bridge when we got to it.

"Think we can wade it?" I shout. "Packs on our heads."

Ken grimaces and rubs a thick black beard. In a former life he must have been a sea captain, one of those salty eighteenth-century sailors who chose water over land. In this life he fled the flat dry lake of northeast Texas for the rough, snow-drifted seas of the Rockies. He spent fifteen seasons as a river guide. Wildwater runs in his veins.

"Won't happen!" he yells. "You'll be tumbled head over heels. If you aren't lucky enough to be drowned, you'll be smashed on the rocks." He twists his tall, wiry frame and points downstream to where the roiling current is slamming into a stone wall.

"Think we could maybe swim it? Tied to the rope."

Ken strokes his beard. He has a mind as eclectic as the library of an Arctic sailing vessel, a memory for ingenious outdoor lore, and a knack for the quintessential quote.

"Excellent way to avoid the rocks," Ken yells, "and ensure a mercifully swift drowning."

We drop the packs in the willows and begin bushwhacking up and down the river, searching for a safe ford. An hour later we're hunting for a ford of any kind. Upstream the river catapults out of a steepwalled gorge; downstream it vanishes into snaking narrows. After we've traversed a hundred miles of glaciers and granite peaks, it's Mother Nature's practical joke to rimrock us with a river swollen by snowmelt.

Ken and I squat on our packs and share a bar of Swiss chocolate. Across the bounding waves, on the opposite shore, we can see the trail rising out of the water.

"An hour down that trail is the car," Ken says.

"An hour in the car to the Lander Bar," I reply.

As is apropos, we started this journey in the Lander Bar, the LB as it's called, a classic Wyoming saloon where bloody-knuckled cowboys and climbers, Arapahoe Indians in beads and braids, granola girls in beads and braids, outcasts, poseurs, foreigners, and the occasional pair of cross-country skiers all drink and dance together.

I can taste the beer and hear the band. Ken catches me studying a large cottonwood hanging out over the water. Opposite the cottonwood, on the far bank, is a forty-foot undercut cliff that resembles the prow of a ship. A span of only ten feet separates the uppermost limbs of the tree from the edge of the cliff.

"Oh no," says Ken, "I know that grin."

"We carried that pretty rope the whole way and never got to use it."

He shakes his head and stands up. "I'll do one last recon further downriver before we commit ourselves."

Everything depends on your perspective. Obstacles look different from different angles. Maybe it's not thirty feet of raging brown water we have to get across, but merely three or four yards of dreamy blue sky.

This trip didn't quite start in the Lander Bar, although that's the last place we were seen alive. And it didn't really start when Ken and I clipped into the bindings, shouldered the packs, and set out to ski the northern half of the Wind River Mountains of Wyoming. The obvious beginning is never the beginning; it's usually the middle. You only recognize the beginning later on, once you've gained some elevation. Once you stop, take off your skis, climb a big rock, and look back. In this case, the beginning was almost twenty years ago, before Ken and I even met.

I was living in a log cabin at 11,000 feet in the Medicine Bow Mountains; Ken was struggling to make a go of a tiny outdoor shop down on the plains. It was a winter of deep snow. My mornings were spent at a typewriter struggling to become a writer; in the afternoons I skied for miles. Ken skied in the morning and spent his afternoons renting cross-country skis and selling outdoor gear. We were in poverty, supposedly—our combined incomes couldn't have bought a bicycle—but who cares when you're outside 300 days a year?

I don't remember how we met—ski touring somewhere—but by spring we'd hatched a plan to become cross-country ski instructors. We drove down to Steamboat and pitched a tent in the snow (all the other prospective instructors stayed in the lodge). At lunch we used our skis for a backrest, drank snowmelt from our water bottles, and ate cold bean burritos (everybody else dined beside the fireplace in the lodge). We weren't stoic, we were broke.

After a week two rubes from Wyoming somehow managed to become certified Nordic instructors. Ken was the better skier—his diagonal stride more graceful, his skating technique cleaner, his telemark turn stronger. However, before the test I'd been certain my navigational skills were superior. I was the mountaineer, I was the one living in the mountains—and I was the one who flunked this test.

Perhaps, at the time, in our hearts, we do have an inkling that we're only just beginning, but we don't want to admit it. We can't. To admit that would be to admit you don't know what you're doing, which would be to admit that you have a long way to go, which would make the journey appear so daunting as to stymie even starting out. Better to believe you know what you're doing and keep doing it until you do.

For the next few winters Ken and I taught Nordic classes and guided backcountry tours. I kept at my writing and he kept at his outdoor store on the outskirts of town. We each kept notes, made adjustments, developed systems, started recognizing what mattered and what didn't. This is how you hone your craft, one detail at a time. Ken collected bad checks, I collected rejection letters. It took years for our passions to pay the rent. Every summer, like migrating birds, I fled for foreign continents and Ken decamped for Idaho to be a river guide. (At different times, we both gave living in the East a try—for the same reason everybody does this: money. And we both wised up after a year or two. Too many trees. When you're trying to figure out where you're going, you need to be able to see the landscape. Trees get in the way.) After a decade Ken moved his shop into a big space downtown and I bought a computer and we both quit drinking Schlitz.

During the next decade we each broke a leg three-pin skiing. I performed a splendid piroutte and twisted my foot right off my leg; Ken sailed dashingly off a cornice and snapped his femur off at the hip. I was high on morphine with a plate and six screws in my leg when he smuggled a six-pack of beer into my prohibition-proud Salt

Lake City hospital. Three years later, Ken's lanky leg in agonizing traction, I waltzed in with a six-pack and a smile. Rehab is hell, but you learn who your friends are.

Through the years Ken became a consummate outdoor athlete. A kayaker, climber, skier. The unassuming outdoorsman, quiet and clear about his knowledge and ability. They are all over the world now. Glenwood Springs, Zermatt, Cuzco. It's a subculture. Men and women who consciously choose the outdoor life. Not for the fame, not for the money, for the life. For the full-moon ski tours and the friends and the dawns when the color of the river is some breath-catching, transcendental blue. They are masters of their craft, but you'd never know it. They aren't in any TV videos or manufacturer's ads or magazine stories.

But Ken and I never did a big trip together. After all those years the idea of skiing the Winds came out of nowhere—spontaneous combustion—the way all the best trips are conceived. One minute we were talking about how to earn enough money to have the life we had when we didn't make a dime, the next minute we were poring over topos.

The goal was to go as light as possible without turning the trip into a sufferfest (no tent, no stove, no fun). Light and fast. Lightning-fast: the one-size-fits-all mantra for mountain travel you either figure out, or you better go back to bowling. We thought the trip would take eight days, including (since we'd be in the neighborhood) a speed-ascent of 13,804-foot Gannett, the highest peak in Wyoming. We wanted our packs to be under forty pounds—which meant no storm rations, no radio, no food drop, no pulp fiction, no extra fuel, no extra clothes, no extra nada. Word of our plan naturally brought out the naysayers.

A veteran instructor from the nearby NOLS (National Outdoor Leadership School) told us it would be so cold we'd need forty-below sleeping bags, expedition parkas, and crates of fuel—so much gear we'd be forced to man-haul sleds. (Think Scott in the Antarctic.) Having spent our share of sixteen-hour nights trapped in January snow-caves, we chose to do our winter trip in summer—mid-June to be exact. Twice the daylight, three times the temp, half the pain. No mosquitoes.

A fellow backcountry skier said we would be killed by avalanches. The snowpack was 200 percent of normal. Weaving through the high peaks would be running a deadly gauntlet. Ken booked us a ride in a souped-up Cessna 172 and we flew the length of our route, spotting and carefully noting only the occasional point-release slide.

A glaciologist said that in June the crevasses could be wide open, waiting to swallow the unwary. We'd have to carry a mountain of mountaineering gear to be safe. (Think Everest.) From the flyover, most of the crevasses appeared to be filled in, so we forsook climbing ropes for a one-pound, 100-foot section of 5mm Kevlar cord; swapped harnesses, pickets, ice screws, deadmen, and all other winter ironmongery for three slings, three biners, and two finger-size ascenders apiece; traded heavy steel ice axes and crampons for their aluminum cousins.

A gearhead said we'd need fat telemark skis, big plastic boots, and heavy cable bindings to negotiate the steep terrain, all of which would demolish our ridiculously optimistic predictions for daily mileage. We took lean, short, featherweight skis and wore Nordic boots. (Think Amundsen in the Antarctic.)

Ken and I did a quick shakedown trip, testing and tweaking, then took off for our ski traverse of the Winds, stopping in the Lander Bar en route.

Day one: Got lost immediately upon leaving Elkhart Park. Took bearings, found ourselves. Snow was sugar with a hard crust. Skis plunged to the ground. Camped on snow, cooked on rock. Strange to think all these deep blue drifts end up in Scottsdale swimming pools.

Day two: Exited timber at 10,200 and the world exploded. Blazing white slopes, towers of gleaming granite, a sea of bright sky. 360-degree views. Reason we came. Camped just over Indian Pass on Knife Point Glacier. Already pack buckles have broken, zippers jammed, boots blistered and bruised our feet. A pox on all designers who've never field-tested their abysmal creations.

Day three: Hit our stride. Crossing passes, banging one glacier after another—Bull Lake, Upper Fremont, Sacagawea, Helen. Big storm climbing Elsie Col. Cloud-cracking lightning, thunder, rain, sleet, hail, graupel, fog, couldn't see each other but kept climbing. Bad weather is psychological. Camped now on Dinwoody Glacier, Gannett above but invisible in storm.

Day four: Moving at four-thirty. Half of successful mountain climbing is an alpine start. Ignored darkness, whiteout, wind, kicked steps straight up Gooseneck Couloir sans rope, summited in two hours. From the summit of Gannett we could see where we had come from and where we were going. You need elevation for perspicuity. If anybody ever asks, this is the reason human beings climb mountains.

Pushed north that afternoon. Cold hard rain for hours. Crossed Gannett Glacier, Dinwoody Glacier, so hypothermic forced to stop. Stove fired up inside tent turned it into a steam room. Stripped to underwear, slept wet, but we're two days ahead of schedule!

Day five: Perfect synchronization now. Triangulate exact position, take bearings to the degree, plot course, circle summits, and slide into passes without gaining or losing altitude. Such joy in navigating when you know what you're doing. Stayed at 13,000 feet, smack on Divide, knocked out twenty-five miles.

Day six: A thousand telemark turns off Shale Mountain and we did it! Dropped into dense forest. Map and compass useless. Postholed for hours. Forded unnamed streams, Wasson Creek, then came Jakey's Fork. Whoajesus.

While Ken is downriver I climb clear to the top of the cottonwood thinking it might be possible to Tarzan from the uppermost branches over to the cliff. It's not. The limbs stop in midair. I shimmy back down.

I get out the 5mm cord, slings, and biners for the first time. I hitch one end of the rope to a twelve-foot log, then reclimb the tree with the other end. Using one sling and two biners I rig a crude winch in the tree, clip the cord in, and drop the end. Then I wait for Ken, swaying in the branches above the crashing rapids. He returns in half an hour and spots me up in the tree. He knew that's where I'd be. He didn't find a ford. I was hoping he wouldn't.

"All we need to do is lift the log up into the top of the tree," I yell, "drop one end into the highest fork," I point to a limb way above me, "and swing the other end over onto the cliff."

"That's all?"

For the next two hours we're like kids building a treehouse. Using carabiners and knots, me crotch-to-crotch up in the tree and Ken down on the ground, we slowly winch the log up into the cotton-wood. We have to reset the rigging several times, once almost losing the log, but eventually we yard the bridge into the sky. With the cot-tonwood rocking in the wind and the log swinging dangerously in midair, Ken muscling the cord from below, me precariously balanced in the arms of the tree, we gently guide the timber into position. Closer, closer . . .

"Drop it!" I bellow.

Voilà. Only six inches of the log rest on the distant lip of the cliff, and the log shifts with each gust, but we've done it.

It was my idea, so it is my duty to go first. Ken gives me a belay from the ground: I loop the cord over a limb and step out onto the log. I gingerly walk the plank. The roar of the river fills the empty air. I can feel the dark water rushing far below. Step. Step. Forget where you are, focus on where you're going.

When I reach the cliff, relief forces a wail of delight from my lungs. Down below on the opposite bank, Ken is giving me the thumbs-up and cheering.

After we send the packs and skis over, Ken ties into the cord. He methodically climbs the tree and, with no hesitation, like a trapeze artist without an audience, tiptoes across the suspension bridge. When he reaches my side he knocks me over in a bear hug.

While I coil the rope Ken builds a cairn and writes a note to put beneath the top stone: "Cowboys beware, this is not a horse crossing."

We heave on our packs and head down the trail. In one hour we hit the car; in two, the Lander Bar, where, naturally, we meet three Kenyan mountain guides working for NOLS. They're listening to the band, watching cowboys trying to two-step to the blues. We pull up stools and one of the Kenyans, in an elegant East African British accent, asks why our faces are so sunburned.

Ken buys pints all around and settles in to tell the story. I push back, relax, close my eyes, and listen to his voice meld with the music. Suddenly I see him. It was just yesterday but it already seems like months ago. He's out in front of me, silhouetted on the horizon, a tiny black figure gliding into an enormous white landscape. I watch him stop, take a bearing, and then, in total silence, continue to glide onward.

It occurs to me that the trips you hear too little about are the ones that work. The journeys where no one dies, no one gets hurt. Friends get together, make a plan, execute the plan, have a grand time, come home. The competence and acumen of the participants match the ferocity of the elements and the challenge of the landscape. People are making such journeys every day, all over the world.

When Ken finishes his tale the Kenyans share one of their own about the rescue of some fools on Kilimanjaro and another about the death of a novice who fell into a moulin, a hole in a glacier, and was never found. We swap stories until last call. The Lander Bar is closing, our trip is over, the end.

Ah, but the end is never the end, it's the middle too. Cross one stream and there's another one just ahead. As we're walking out one of the Kenyans grabs my arm.

"I know another place quite difficult to get into," he tells me. "It too is high and remote, but it's in the heart of Africa."

Endangered Species

Douré is striding along the edge of the escarpment, a thin figure silhouetted against the lavender dawn. He is nimble, his pace swift and economical. A Kalashnikov is slung from one shoulder, carried easily, almost as if it were not real. The path arcs along the curve of the precipice, a 3,000-foot drop just inches away, but Douré is surefooted, singing quietly to himself, insouciant. This dry, deeply riven country is his homeland.

We are hiking through the Simien Mountains of northern Ethiopia. Douré, our armed scout, Mulat, our guide, my wife, Sue, and me.

The first look over the escarpment, even if one is accustomed to the vertigo of mountains, is shocking. In a nanosecond the eyes gauge the fantastic drop, the mind imagines the plummet to death, instinct secretes a warning into the blood and the body recoils.

There are chasms of air beside us. The scalloped rim presents a series of sheer walls ahead and behind, but to our left there is an utter falling away, a dropping and dropping until a dissected badlands finally looms up. The black shadow of the escarpment cuts jaggedly across the netherworld far below.

"It's like the Grand Canyon," says Sue. "Like looking off the South Rim without a North Rim on the other side."

Douré and Mulat stop and pass the binoculars back and forth, glassing the walls. They are searching for ibex. They find nothing and we continue along the escarpment. The trail drops down a hundred feet, paralleling the scythelike curve of the canyon rim, then begins ascending.

There is something ahead of us on the trail: a shaggy mane silhouetted against the skyline.

"Lion baboon," Mulat whispers.

We move forward in a crouch, halting behind a bush. It is a troop of baboons, perhaps fifty in all. They are warming themselves in the morning sun, picking lice from each other's fur, cavorting, chewing handfuls of grass.

"Gelada baboons," Mulat says. "We name them lion baboons, or bleeding hearts."

The males have great lionlike manes of tawny fur. "Bleeding heart" refers to a distinctive triangle of bare pink flesh on the chests of both males and females. Unlike baboons in other parts of Africa, lion baboons are afraid of humans. As soon as Sue and I try to approach, the dominant males curl their lips back and bare their teeth. We freeze immediately, but now they are agitated. The males are nervously cocking their heads. They begin to scream. It's a signal— suddenly every animal in the troop flies to the edge of the precipice and flings itself off.

We're speechless. It seems they have committed suicide en masse. I spring to the edge, drop to my hands and knees, and peer over the rim. I expect to see several dozen primates flailing down through thin air.

Instead, they are all perched on tiny ledges along the sheer face of the cliff. I can't understand how they have landed safely. Then one of the baboons spots my white face. Shrieks echo along the cliffs and the entire troop again leaps into space—revealing their fabulous secret.

Each baboon vaults into midair, allows itself a free fall of ten or twenty feet, then reaches out impossibly powerful hands, grabs hold of tufts of grass, and gracefully swings itself back into the cliff. It is the most dazzling display of agility and sangfroid I have ever seen in my life.

The Simien Mountains stretch from east to west across the far north of Ethiopia, seventy-five miles south of Eritrea, 100 miles east of Sudan, 350 miles west of the Red Sea. The range is actually a wildly incised plateau with a vertical, north-facing escarpment.

The Simiens have had a battlement view of the interminable war between Ethiopia and Eritrea. In 1962 Ethiopia attempted to absorb Eritrea, precipitating a thirty-one-year civil war. Although Eritrea eventually prevailed, declaring itself an independent state in 1993, sporadic fighting continued. Last July a cease-fire was negotiated, and in December, Eritrea and Ethiopia finally signed a peace treaty. No one knows if it will last.

Since working as a newspaper reporter in Kenya in the mid-1980s, I had been dreaming of a trek in northern Ethiopia. For the Simien Mountains, one of the most striking ranges in all of Africa, are not only home to an enclave of ancient Amharic farmers, but they are also one of the last pinpricks of habitat left for three endangered mammals: the gelada baboon, the walia ibex, and the Simien wolf.

Gelada baboons and their relatives once roamed the African savanna from Ethiopia south to the Cape; today they live only in the Afro-alpine ecological zone of Ethiopia. They are the only primates in the world that subsist on grass, and they have more manual dexterity than any monkey on earth.

The walia ibex exist only in or near the miniature (sixty-nine-square-mile) Simien National Park. The walls of the escarpment are their final redoubt. At last count, only about 400 animals remain.

As for the Simien wolf, it is one of the rarest and most endangered canids on the planet. There are none in captivity; the total population in the wild is less than 500. No more than fifty and perhaps far fewer individuals survive in their namesake range.

The spillover effects of war, coupled with overpopulation, disease, and poverty—the Four Horsemen of the Apocalypse that have ravaged so much of Africa—have left the wildlife in the Simien

Mountains balanced on the brink of oblivion. In 1996, the United Nations designated the park as an endangered World Heritage Site, and it is one of the few places on the planet that desperately need foreign visitors—their money and their encouragement.

A month after the peace treaty was signed, Sue and I flew to Ethiopia.

We arrived in the dust-choked village of Debark after two days of flights and four hours in a grinding local bus. The headquarters of the Simien Mountains National Park is a tin-roofed bungalow on a steep hillside.

The cost for a week of trekking in the park for two hikers—plus a scout, a guide, a muleteer, and two pack animals (all mandatory)—was roughly $200. An hour after we paid, our packs were already cinched onto two small, slight Ethiopian horses; our white-turbaned muleskinner–cum–holy man had murmured prayers for the safety of our journey; Mulat had filled his army canteen with water; Douré had filled his clip with thirty shiny bullets; and we were off.

The trail sliced up through an erosional landscape of mesas and gorges where the bird life was stunning.

"Over 830 species in Ethiopia," said Mulat, "sixteen endemic to Ethiopia."

Mulat could name every bird we encountered: red-winged starling, blackheaded siskin, kestrel, white-backed vulture, thick-billed raven. I pointed up at an enormous, rufous-colored, sharp-winged raptor circling above us.

"The lammergeier," said Mulat gravely, "the bone bird."

The lammergeier is a mythical creature to the Ethiopians, for it feeds on marrow. Living on the edge of precipices, it will raise skeletons high into the sky, dash them onto the rocks, and then extract the marrow with its curved beak. Legend has it that the lammergeier will sometimes dive at animals, even humans, trying to scare them into falling off the escarpment.

While I walked with Mulat, Sue walked with Douré. The two of them developed an immediate, intuitive rapport. Because Douré did not speak a word of English, Sue practiced her fledgling Amharic.

"*Dehna neh Douré?*" How are you, Douré?

Douré's regal face, very small and chiseled and refined, with pointed cheekbones, a prince's nose and topped by a purple skull cap, crinkled in delight. "*Dehna!*" I am fine. He had the highest voice of any man I'd ever met.

I asked Mulat why Douré carried a machine gun.

"For protection," said Mulat.

"From what?"

"Animals."

"What animals?"

"Leopards," said Mulat.

"Leopards do not attack grown humans," I argued.

"Hyenas."

"Hyenas don't attack humans."

"Okay. Humans," Mulat said finally. "Humans do attack humans."

Who? Rebels left over from the war with Eritrea? Bandits? Opportunists? I was unsure what he meant.

"Are there humans in this park that would attack us?"

"No."

"Then why are we required to hire an armed guard?"

"For protection."

There was no easing into this trek. In four hours we covered twelve miles and gained 3,000 feet. Much of the land was intensely cultivated, a dry quiltwork of barley fields and hayfields and pastures shorn down to the dirt by goats and sheep. When the Simien Mountains National Park was established, in 1969, the region was populated, the plateau thoroughly agrarian. Only the face of the escarpment was free of humans. Encroachment by farmers and livestock was already decimating the park's wildlife. Still, local tribesmen were given the opportunity to work for the park as scouts. Some of their families had lived here for 2,000 years—this was their habitat as well.

On every slope we met shepherds and farmers, their knobby-kneed legs hardly thicker than their canes. Douré greeted all of them. They were his kinsmen and his neighbors and we shook their hands. At dusk, we reached the lip of the escarpment and camped.

The next morning we encountered the flying trapeze troupe of lion baboons. They made such an impression on Sue and me that, while the muleteer and packhorses beelined for the next camp through the tilled fields, we insisted that the four of us hike along the escarpment for the rest of the journey. Because of the denticulated architecture of the rim, with its numerous and perilous lookouts, this would add countless miles to the trip.

Douré was silently skeptical. No *ferenge* (Amharic for "gringo") had ever walked the rim. That trail was for the wild animals, and the locals, people who knew how to walk. But, by the third day, we had proven ourselves.

There is one sure way to gain the respect of a village African: walk with him. NGO workers are chauffeured around in white Land Cruisers. Soldiers roar by in military trucks. The untouchably wealthy blacks and Indians cruise past in Mercedes sedans with tinted windows. But rural Africans walk. Their legs are their life. You can give them food or money or praise or pity and you will hardly get a thank-you. But just once, step out of your automobile and volunteer to walk with them, at their pace for as long as they walk and as far as they walk, without whining or judging or condescending, and you have earned their respect for life.

Ethiopians go only by first names, which often have meaning. Tesfaye means "Hope." Terunesh means "Wonderful." Ababa, "Flower." Halfway through our trek, Douré rechristened Sue "Madame Gobez." Madame Strong.

I was the first to spot the walia ibex. We had left camp before it was light and hiked out to a point called Imet Gogo, the Great Cliff. It is a blade of rock that glides straight out into nothingness. In places it is no more than three feet wide: imagine a long, narrow diving board sticking out from the summit of El Capitan. We cautiously tiptoed to the end and sat down.

We were inside the dawn. The radiating purples and pinks and oranges were not over there, on the horizon, but all around us. We could stick a hand out into it as if the sky were liquid.

I wouldn't have seen them without the monocular—a group of four, one male, with the distinctively tall, black, backward-arching horns, and three females. They had intelligent faces, dark brown coats, and white socks. They were skipping along a sheer face, occasionally leaping into space and landing perfectly balanced on a lower ledge. It didn't seem possible.

They were masterful, almost gay, in their footwork. Springing up or down, trotting along rope-thin trails, wheeling and knocking heads with never less than a thousand-foot death sentence for one mistake.

We watched them, spellbound, until they disappeared around a buttress. Like the baboons, the ibex had somehow learned to defy the odds. We saw three more bands of walia ibex that day, the last of which was so close we could watch their playful bounding with the naked eye.

The last night, we camped outside a village called Gich, a collection of round thatched huts. This was Douré's home. Where he had been born and raised and lived today. Each hut was surrounded by an intricate brush wall. Inside the wall was a carefully tended vegetable garden and a few head-snapping chickens.

We put up the tents and Mulat started a small fire. Just after dark an old woman hobbled into camp. She had gashed her leg splitting fire-wood. By firelight, Sue cleaned the wound and I dressed it. We gave her antiseptic cream and painkillers and she vanished back into the dark.

"That was good of you," Mulat said. "It was not a bad wound, but she is old."

"It was pretty deep."

Mulat shook his head. "That is not deep."

Then Mulat told me how he had been taken from his home by henchmen of the Mengistu regime, beaten, and sent to the Eritrean front. He had survived three years in the trenches. He was only released after being wounded in the leg by shrapnel.

"It was very, very, very bad," he said.

"Did you have friends die?"

"Many, many, so many. It is normal in Ethiopia. In Ethiopia, if you are in army, you die."

"Somehow, you didn't."

Mulat shrugged.

Some minutes later, he said: "It is better to die than be forever damaged. Then you only suffer once."

Later that night, Douré invited Sue and me into his mud hut for dinner. We sat on goat skins in the dark in the wood smoke around a flickering fire. He introduced us to his wife, Taggusunnat—"Patience." She was squatting by the fire wrapped in scarlet cloth, her shoulders draped in a soiled blanket. She was young, a tattoo of a cross on her right temple, lustrous brown eyes. She shook our hands with both of hers without standing up.

We had injera and coffee. Injera is the Ethiopian staple, a platter-size crepe made from teff, a grain similar to couscous. (And coffee, of course, is native to Ethiopia; the word may have derived from the ancient southwestern province of Kefa.) Douré tore off chunks of mud-colored injera while Taggusunnat poured cup after cup of high-octane coffee.

We talked through sign language. Douré is forty-two. Until the age of thirty, he went barefoot. Now, as a scout, he wears plastic sandals. He carries no backpack and wears the same jacket in all weather. He carries no water and only a chunk of bread in his pocket for lunch. He carries the AK-47 but has never fired it. He has never been sent to war. He has never been sick. The Four Horsemen have not yet found him or his wife hiding high in the Simiens.

That night, lying in sleeping bags, Sue and I heard the ululating of the women of Gich, a celebration of some unknown event in the life of the village. The joyful trilling rose and dipped and rose again.

Douré is striding along the escarpment through a lavender dawn. It is the last day of our trek. The trail moves in a straight line down through boulders and across incipient wadis. The stars are vanishing, details in the rugged landscape resurfacing from the depth of night. Douré is humming, Sue and Mulat silent.

We are moving in single file at a distance-devouring clip. Douré's eyes are scanning the horizon when he abruptly stops. His small head spins sideways.

"Ky kebero!" he whispers, his voice as high-pitched as a girl's.

I try to look precisely where he is looking but see nothing. Mulat spots it and points.

Douré swiftly pulls a pair of binoculars from his jacket pocket and hands them to me. I pan, stop, back up to a flicker of motion.

"What is it?" Sue asks.

I see it now. "A wolf!"

The wolf is loping across the plateau, head down, moving quickly. It is a slight, ephemeral figure, more the size of a jackal than a wolf. Reddish fur with flicking white socks. It is bounding over the frosted grass, weaving through the giant lobelia.

I pass the binoculars to Sue.

"Where?"

"Ten o'clock."

She glasses the exact place but sees nothing.

"I am sorry," says Mulat, "*Ky kebero* gone now."

It is then that I remember. I'd completely forgotten: I heard them last night.

At first the distant yipping and howling had been in my dreams and, beginning to wake, I'd thought I invented it. That is what you can do in dreams—create a world you wish existed. But then the choral yelping had separated from the hypnopompic images and I realized that the singing was real, echoing in the surrounding darkness.

I'd pulled my arm out of the warm sleeping bag and pressed the light on my watch. Four-fifteen. I'd lain back and listened. The faint call and response and refrain, like a faraway psalmody in some ancient language, had cheered me immensely. Somehow, through everything, they were still alive. They were out there, even if we never saw them.

ICONOCLASTS

Pickles

We were discussing the accident again, trying to figure out how it could have happened. It was early morning and though the highway was striped with sunlight, the bush was as black as ever.

"Maybe one of 'em was injured," said Rick, sitting up front in the passenger seat. "Hit by falling rock."

"There's to be an inquest," said Derek, the driver. "And autopsies."

Three days earlier, on June 14, the accident had made the front page of the Sydney Morning Herald: "Two experienced abseilers froze to death in a wilderness waterfall in the Blue Mountains after their ropes became entangled, leaving them trapped and dangling against a steep escarpment as night set in." The article went on to thinly outline a three-day canyoning adventure that had been advertised on the Web site of the Newcastle University Mountaineering Club as a trip with "more abseils than you can poke a piton at." The story was accompanied by a large photograph of helicopters hovering against a cliff face above a green forest, like dragonflies above a garden.

"They died on Corra Beanga Falls," said Derek, turning off onto a narrow dirt road. "You've done that haven't you, Rick?"

"That'n. Yes, I 'ave."

At last count, Rick Jamieson, fifty-nine, had descended some 200 canyons in the Blue Mountains of Australia. He wrote the book on canyoning Down Under, Canyons Near Sydney, now in its third edition. He made his first technical descent in 1961, two decades before canyoneering, or canyoning, as a sport would develop in the deserts of the Western U.S. A big rock of a man—thick in the hands and feet, with curly gray hair, a grizzled beard, a heavy Aussie accent, and an uncanny resemblance to the late British explorer-mountaineer H. W. Tilman—Rick tended to think more than he spoke.

Derek Cannon is Rick's canyoning partner. They've done most of the canyons in his guidebook together. Derek, sixty-two, is a retired limnologist who worked for the Sydney Water Authority for thirty-three years while simultaneously rising from private to lieutenant colonel in the Australian army reserve. He's trim, indefatigable, and has led trekking expeditions around the world.

Derek and Rick go canyoning forty-plus weekends a year. We were driving to Bennett Gully, a small, virtually unknown slot canyon that had never been descended. Bouncing in the back seat, I kept brooding about the two dead canyoneers.

"They must not really have been experienced," I said.

Derek held the wheel steady and glanced at me in the rearview mirror. Rick didn't look back.

"They must have made stupid mistakes," I said.

"Or," Rick said, shrugging his shoulders, "'ey might 'ave just made a simple error in judgment."

Geography is destiny. Australia's Blue Mountains are ideal for canyoning because they aren't, in fact, mountains at all, but rather a long sandstone plateau riven with gorges—an incised geography of 500-foot cliffs, steep talus, and crayfish creeks all buried beneath what Aussies call "bush" and we would call rain forest. Gorgeous, pale-skinned blue gums, ferns the size of fountains, fens of eight-foot razor grass, shawls of green moss on every stone and steep wall. Imagine a bony Utah fleshed over by Louisiana foliage so dense all the slot canyons are hidden beneath a python's nest of roots. Most slot canyons here don't even show up on maps; Rick decried topos as "bloody useless."

The Blue Mountains rise like a wave just west of Sydney. Sydney: the beach-blond antipodal sister of raven-haired San Francisco, with a better port, a bigger gay pride parade, cleaner streets, swimable seas, and a week of sun for every day of rain.

June in Australia is winter, putatively the wrong season for canyoning. I'd been warned by a vocal American canyoneer that it would be impossible to go canyoning in June. "You'll freeze to death!" he warned hysterically. When I mentioned this to Rick in our first phone conversation, he said something that sounded like "aaar-rruhhgg," then grumbled about "bloody whingey Americans." I bought a ticket.

(Thank God for earth's vestigial incorrigibles, the outdoor atavists, the few who still go outside in all seasons. Hate to say it, but there aren't many left in the U.S.—many good men having devolved into fair-weather adventurers. In Australia, perhaps due to its isolation, the breed is still thriving.)

The morning Rick turned up to drive me out to do our first canyon (Derek was busy that day) it was snowing in the Snowy Mountains, south of the capital, and newscasters were calling the weather "bittah cold." The city people were hiding inside winter coats and wool scarves. Rick was wearing exactly what you'd expect of a man whom one local canyoneer described as a "fokkin legend": ratty sweater, threadbare khaki shorts, flattened sneakers.

Rick is one of those old-school bush veterans who live in shorts. Long pants are anathema to him. So too a coat of any kind. "The best plan is to wear a woollen jumper next to the skin," he writes in *Canyons Near Sydney*. Same goes for the misery of heavy hiking boots: "We recommend Volley sandshoes [cheap canvas sneakers], as they are quite good on slippery rocks."

Brushing aside the beer cans in the back of his station wagon, I saw that his backpack was no better: a potato-shaped lump of such great age and abuse that all the buckles were gone and the nylon fabric, stitched and restitched, worn to fuzz. Crammed in with the rest of his gear and supplies was a dark, unidentifiable object.

"What's that?"

"Whut? Me wet suit?"

Although still vaguely blue, it resembled some ragged animal skin, with the sleeves cut off at the biceps and legs cut off above the thighs. Most appalling, the crotch was ripped from belly button to tailbone.

"That keeps you warm?"

"Nah," said Rick sheepishly, "caun't say that it does. But I brought me balaclava."

I took all this as a good sign. The older the gear, the better. People with new gear scare me: the scanty wear-and-tear of their equipage is too often indicative of the scantiness of their experience, which means you don't want to go on a hike with them, let alone descend into the orifices of the earth.

That day we did a canyon called Yileen, an Aborigine word for "dream." It had numerous rappels that dropped straight into icy ebony pools.

"There go me family jewels!" Rick would howl, then rapidly half-wade, half-swim down the penumbral corridor and stumble up onto the next sandbank, chortling. I was wearing an intact wet suit and it was still bone-chilling.

By the time we got to the final rap, a stunning 200-foot drop alongside a vaporous waterfall, our feet were wooden blocks and our fingers rubber bananas. It took an hour of hiking fast and hard uphill with packs to warm up. Rick declared the day "a beauty."

One good measure of an adventurer is how he acts when he is uncomfortable. Does he whine, keep quiet, or revel? The former is unforgivable, the second acceptable, the last admirable.

That night we sat close to the woodstove in Rick's home at the edge of the Blue Mountains and drank hot tea. After some prodding

Rick told me about a 950-mile canoe trip he made down the Mackenzie River in Canada right after getting his Ph.D. in electrical engineering and marrying Jane (pronounced "yana"), his Danish wife.
That somehow led to another adventure that he inexplicably referred
to as "the fahs."

"Fahs?" I said.

"Yap. F.A.R.C.E. Fantastical Australian Rock Climbing Expedition.
Nineteen seventy-two. Six months. Drove a combi from Denmark to
Australia, right through bloody Asia." Rick stretched his muscled legs,
which, if it weren't for the lumps and scars and half-century tan,
could belong to an Olympic runner. "Wanted to climb a mountain in
Afghanistan, an' almost did."

Yileen was just a warm-up. A chance for Rick to see if I cut the mustard.

"Got one!" he said one morning, as if snatching a trout from a
stream, "Canyon's called Oronga." Which inaptly means "sleep" in
the Aborigine language.

No one had successfully completed a descent of Oronga. Even
today in our nothing's-left-everything's-been-done world, the Blue
Mountains are still not explored out. No matter that they're a mere
two-hour train ride from four million people. Five years earlier, Rick
and some mates had attempted Oronga but had been turned back by
a drop so deep they couldn't see the bottom.

"Was one a 'em misty mornin's," Rick said, "an' the stream fell
over the cliff and just vanished into the clouds."

So it was, on another freezing, misty morning, that Rick and I
attempted Oronga Canyon. The descent started with a short rappel
through overhanging vines, followed by another rap from a tree limb
into a black abyss. Down inside Oronga we followed one passageway
after another, each as dark and dank as a dungeon, before crawling
out atop a series of enormous, undercut cliff bands. It took four con-

secutive rappels—never knowing if we might get stranded halfway down a wall—before we reached the bottom of the canyon. We'd done it . . . almost. In fact, the hike out turned into a grueling bushwhack. Forced to struggle our way through miles of thorn-spiked vines, by the end, Rick's legs were so severely gouged and scratched I could follow the drips of blood through the forest. Still, eight hours after we'd started, we were back at the car.

"Whut a bahgain," roared Rick, tossing me a beer from behind the seat.

During the hike out I learned that Rick had been a freelance computer programmer since the dawn of the damn machines. "Don't like to work more'n couple days a week." Which left time for raising two sons and one daughter, voluminous reading, and writing books on subjects other than canyoning, including *A Religion Without a God* (a treatise on the faith of atheists) and *Let's Spel Lojicly: Wi stic tu the hard old way ov spelling?* (an argument for the simplification of English orthography). He had also managed to lead thirteen trekking expeditions to the Himalayas, climb the Matterhorn twice, and drive overland from Munich to Cape Town.

"We got 'rselves into heaps of pickles in Africa. Mighty! Spent a whole month in jail in the Congo. 'Ey thought we were bloody mercenaries. Ten days in a hole in Brazzaville, and then shipped down the big river—pygmies would paddle out and give us bananas—to Pointe Noire, where we spent another three weeks in jail before gettin' out. At any one time we were always in at least two pickles. Tryin' to get 'rselves out of one of 'em while straight away pulling 'rselves into another."

The three of us stepped out of the car above Bennett Gully and looked at the map. Derek was outfitted just like Rick: wool sweater, shorts, Volleys.

Dropping into the head of the canyon, we were instantly engulfed by bush and began creeping through tunnels of vegetation, one after another, sometimes wading through the water, sometimes balancing along a latticework of deadfall suspended like a bridge above the streambed. When the brambles became impassable, we would scrabble up the canyon sidewalls and work our way along slopey, discontinuous ledges.

Slithering, clambering, and clawing through bush—literally bushwhacking—is distinctive to Blue Mountain canyoning. To be a good canyoneer here, you must be a great bushwalker. It was instructive to watch how gracefully Rick and Derek tiptoed along the alligator backs of logs, contorted through cobwebs of vines, and leapt rock to rock. As a team we were as efficient as guerrillas, the man in front rotating as each of us ran into vegetal cul-de-sacs and advised the two behind to find a different path. At any drop, or whenever we got rimrocked, the point man would already have a rope ready by the time the other two arrived.

We were down in the dark, passing from one chamber to the next, when, right in front of us, sky appeared. A brilliant wedge of blue between two black walls. The stream at our feet rushed toward the drop-off, pooled in a cleft as if psyching itself up, then slowly slid over the edge like a suicide jumper who has second thoughts a second too late.

We took turns stepping carefully to the lip, hanging on to a limb and looking down. It was a tremendous drop. The rock was undercut and the stream came apart falling through the emptiness. The yawning space made Derek cock his head like an officer, Rick squint, and my nuts involuntarily contract.

A hundred feet down and to the right there was a long ledge. Unfortunately, below it we could see nothing but blank walls.

"She may not go," said Rick. "After the ledge it's a hell of a long ways to the ground an' looks like there's nothin' for abseils."

I volunteered to check it out. Reaching the ledge required traversing a fragile trellis of branches suspended in space—something akin to crawling out onto a lilac bush drooping off the side of a fifty-story building—which I managed, barely. On the ledge I hung out as far as I could in different places, searching the walls below. Unless I found something from which to set up another rappel, the descent was over: I would have to jug back up the rope and we would be forced to somehow back out of Bennett Gully.

I was about to give up when I spotted something beautiful: a dead tree. A slender, limbless, blackened trunk leaning out of a seam. I immediately rappelled down to it and attached myself. I was now two ropes below Rick and Derek.

"It'll go!" I yelled up, exhilarated.

Rick's voice was barely audible. "Will . . . the . . . ropes . . . reach . . . the . . . bottom?"

Looking straight down it's hard to judge distance. I studied the surrounding cliff faces vanishing into the forest. Our ropes were 200 feet long. It couldn't be more than 200 feet more to the bottom.

"Yeesss . . ."

I wasn't sure. I thought they would reach. It was a judgment call.

"Abseiling!"

Rick and Derek rapped down to the ledge, pulled the ropes, set up the next rappel, and started down again.

The one foolproof way to get yourself killed in a canyon is to get stranded halfway. If it starts to rain, you'll either be drowned, swept over the cliffs, or die of exposure. Even if it doesn't rain, but you're wet and the temperature drops, or the wind picks up and blows the waterfall over you and you subsequently become wet, you'll be popsicled in a matter of hours.

The one foolproof way to get stuck halfway is to pull your ropes down from above, eliminating all chance of retreat, only to find that they won't reach the bottom. Unlike in mountaineering, where you can usually turn around at almost any point, serious canyoning is a one-way trip. Once you pull your ropes, the only way out, the only way back home, is down.

Derek and Rick completed their descent and pulled the ropes. Then we were all three hanging from a small dead tree in the middle of a remote cliff face in the middle of the Blue Mountains. We knotted the ropes through a sling I'd tied around the tree, and dropped them.

They dove down through space, and stopped. They didn't reach. I couldn't believe it. We could see the ends dangling in midair, snapping lazily like tiger tails, the forest floor still somewhere far below.

"They're really close," I said.

"Fair dinkum," said Rick. "We get down there and we'll be laughin'."

Derek chuckled.

"You have the extra short rope, right, Rick?" I was trying to sound imperturbable. They knew what I was about to suggest: tie the short rope permanently to the dead tree, put a loop in the end, and hang the long ropes through the loop. It would require a mid-wall transfer from the fixed rope to the double, a dangerous maneuver, but it would give us an extra thirty feet or more.

"Tricky," said Rick, obviously pleased.

"If it doesn't reach . . ." Derek shrugged and didn't finish his sentence.

We rerigged the ropes and I went first. Down the single line, making the transfer onto the double; then came a great swing out into midair several hundred feet above the earth, something that always gives one a minor synaptic shock. As I slid down the ropes, fifteen feet out from the overhanging wall, I still couldn't tell if they reached the ground. Near the bottom the ends were coiled in the top of a tree. I anxiously descended through the forest canopy to the very end of the rope. I was ten feet from the ground.

Close enough. I dropped.

"The . . . ropes . . . reach!"

Derek let out a battle cry and swung into space.

When Rick reached the ground he looked up and said, laconic as ever, "That dead tree. She won't be there for long."

By twilight we were walking through the tall grass between the ghostly blue gums. It began to rain and Rick and Derek started singing "April Showers," the Al Jolson tune. Then a cold night set in and it began to pour.

In the Good Company
of the Dead

So George Mallory, perhaps the most famous mountaineer in history, has been found. Lost on Mount Everest on June 8, 1924, his body was discovered by the Mallory & Irvine Research Expedition in early May 1999.

By now everyone has seen the at once macabre and glorious photo of Mallory high on the north face of Everest: his fingers still clenched in a death grip with the mountain, head bent in determination, leg broken, clothes ripped from his torso exposing his back to a lashing from the wind. Oddly, Mallory's bare back is unmarked, as milky and muscled as the back of Michelangelo's David. With faith and hubris, woefully underequipped for a battle at high altitude, armed with little more than a length of rope, a straight-picked axe, and hobnailed boots, Mallory, the Brit who, for better or worse, gave climbing its most famous koan, "Because it's there"—set out to scale the highest peak on the planet, and perished in the attempt.

Did he, with or without his climbing partner, Andrew Irvine, reach the 29,028-foot summit of Everest twenty-nine years before Hillary and Tenzing? Or did he die trying? In mountaineering circles these have been the great imponderables for three generations, and we still don't know the answer. Definitive evidence—film from a Kodak Vest Pocket camera that Mallory was said to be carrying—was not found. Betting on a long shot, this spring's Mallory & Irvine Research Expedition successfully added large pieces to the puzzle, but the mystery remains.

When the news broke my first response was surprise tinged with admiration. I'd spoken to expedition leader Eric Simonson before his departure, and he'd been cautiously optimistic about its goals. Having attempted the north face of Everest myself, I'd been hopeful but skeptical about their chances of finding much. The bold deserve their luck.

My second response was dread: once again, mountaineering and its beleaguered poster child, Everest, would be shoved into the limelight. Once again, ambulance-chasing journalists and callow blab show hosts would suddenly be expounding fatuously and fallaciously on the meaning of mountaineering. Others also felt this fear and loathing. For some the photo alone was a measure of how low the press would stoop to entertain the ghoulish voyeurism of the public.

"I'm absolutely appalled by this," said the great sixty-five-year-old British mountaineer Sir Chris Bonington. "Words can't express how disgusted I am." Audrey Salkeld, co-author of *The Mystery of Mallory and Irvine*, said, "I'm horrified it's got to this stage." Given that Bonington has assiduously courted the media his entire career, and Salkeld is a consultant for the very production company making a documentary about Mallory—and all proceeds from the sale of the photo are going to Himalayan charities—such responses struck me as unconsidered but understandable: a visceral disgust in the face of what appeared to be the sensationalizing and thus trivializing of Mallory's accomplishments and fate.

Expecting the worst, I fired up the computer to read the real-time reports on Mountainzone.com, one of the sponsors of the Mallory & Irvine Research Expedition. "Our expedition was formed to pay homage to these great British climbers," wrote Simonson, "and I can only say again that I have always revered the world's brave explorers, and that I am humbled and honored to be able to lead this expedition and the climbers on this team who are responsible for this discovery."

Conrad Anker, the climber who found the body, said Mallory seemed "at peace with himself . . . there was something very, very subtle about his being there, not really scary and violent."

"The image that'll stick in my mind forever," wrote alpinist Andy Politz, "is of a man fighting for his life right to the very end."

I was taken aback. The climbers, writing their thoughts in simple unaffected sentences, were to a one gracious and sincere. Here was history without hype. Everest the way it is, not the way it is marketed. Visitors to the Web site's online forum reacted in kind.

"I usually think of the mountains I've climbed as 'tests,'" wrote one climber. "Tests of my physical conditioning. Tests of my spirit. And there's usually been a test of my morality and integrity and depth of friendship that pops up on every outing. These are all things that deserve periodic testing, and climbing is a great way to do that. One doesn't pass any of the above tests without keeping his or her ego reined in pretty tight."

One writer blasted climbing Everest, and by implication climbing in general, as just another ego trip. Two opposite but equally powerful online rebuttals: "Ego shmeego, people do it because it's fun and rewarding." And, "I'm no expert, but I think it's a bit shortsighted to say that it's done for ego . . . explaining why someone dares the difficult is similar to trying to explain why you fall in love or why your heart aches when a loved one leaves . . . just not an easy thing to explain. I also believe that by climbing high mountains or by doing anything adventurous, people contribute to the human experience. It builds humanity's passion to succeed, to grow, to experience new things."

There were hundreds of letters. A few adolescent, a few asinine, but many were as plain and poignant as those above. Somehow, even after the 1996 Everest debacle and its never-ending exploitation, most ordinary people still believe that trying to climb Everest is a noble pursuit. After seventy-five years, Mount Everest is still a metaphor of itself.

Which is precisely what it was for Mallory.

From his earliest childhood in the 1890s, George Mallory was a preternatural climber. Growing up in the Cheshire countryside, the minister's son "climbed everything that it was at all possible to climb," recalled his sister, Avie. "I learnt very early that it was fatal to tell him that any tree was impossible for him to get up."

When there were no trees, Mallory climbed buildings. As an adolescent he would slip out windows and traverse tight-mortared British brick—"buildering" three generations before the word was coined. He free-climbed the tower of the Abbey of Romsey and the tower of the Chamber Court of Winchester. Years later, during a lecture tour in America, he was photographed climbing the fire escape of a New York skyscraper upside down.

Born into an upper-middle-class English family in 1886, Mallory attended Winchester College, then Magdalene College in Cambridge. He was a good student but an outstanding athlete who excelled in gymnastics. At Cambridge he grew his hair long, read poetry, studied literature, and escaped to the mountains at every opportunity. He was as handsome as a Greek god and painfully idealistic; among his Cambridge circle of climbers he was called Sir Galahad.

He made his first trip to the Swiss Alps at the age of eighteen and climbed for a month. He got altitude-sick and got over it. He failed on some mountains and succeeded on others. At the time, climbing without a guide was considered reckless. Mallory paid no heed and in the years to come he would return to the Alps again and again. Climbing trips would become a way of life.

"How to get the best of it all?" Mallory wrote in his journal after summiting Mont Blanc in 1911. "One must conquer, achieve, get to the top; one must know the end to be convinced that one can win the end—to know there's no dream that mustn't be dared."

Even if his words strained toward the transcendental, Mallory's innate mastery of movement on rock came effortlessly. "He was prudent, according to his own standards," said one female admirer, "but his standards were not those of the ordinary medium-good rock-climber. The fact was that difficult rocks had become to him a perfectly normal element; his prodigious reach, his great strength, and his admirable technique, joined in a sort of catlike agility, made him feel completely secure on rocks so difficult as to fill less competent climbers with a sense of hazardous enterprise."

"Watching George at work," wrote a friend who climbed with Mallory in Switzerland, "one was conscious not so much of physical strength as of suppleness and balance; so rhythmical and harmonious was his progress in any steep place, above all on slabs, that his movements appeared almost serpentine in their smoothness."

His grace and fluidity are peculiarly telling, for climbing to Mallory was the physical counterbalance to a vigorous intellectual life. Mallory could become intoxicated by the beauty of a collection of Chinese paintings, or debate the merits of Gauguin or Cézanne straight through the night. To Mallory, mountaineering was essentially an aesthetic experience. Climbers "notoriously endanger their lives," he wrote in the Climber's Club Journal in March 1914. "With what object? If only for some physical pleasure, to enjoy certain movements of the body and to experience the zest of emulation, then it is not worthwhile. . . . The only defense for mountaineering puts it on a higher plane than mere physical sensation . . . sunrises and sunsets and clouds and thunder are not incidental to mountaineering, but a vital and inseparable part of it; they are not ornamental, but structural." Later in the same essay he compared a day climbing in the Alps to a symphony. The andante, allegro, and scherzo of a "magnificent frolic" up rock and ice.

When he penned these words Mallory was a teacher at the Charterhouse School in Godalming, regularly dragging his pupils outdoors to discover for themselves the intrinsic link between aesthetics, athletics, and the outdoors. The famous poet Robert Graves was one of his students. "I had never heard of people like Shaw, Samuel Butler, Rupert Brooke, Wells, Flecker, and Masefield," wrote Graves, "and I was greatly interested in them."

In that same year, after just four months of intense epistolary courtship, Mallory married Ruth Turner, a woman of Botticellian beauty. This daughter of an architect who lived across the valley from Charterhouse "saw with great clarity the things that mattered and spoke with sometimes startling honesty," according to Mallory's best biographer, David Robertson. Their first child, Frances Clare, was born a year later. When she was six months old, Mallory went to war.

Mallory was a gunner in the trenches north of Armentières, France. Men were blown apart all around him. Men died of tuberculosis and gangrene. As they would throughout the brief decade of their marriage, Ruth wrote letters to George and George wrote letters to Ruth: "I had a horrible experience yesterday: two of my party killed by a shell on the way back from the trenches. . . . I had no clear idea where the shell exploded, but looked back to see if the two were all right and saw the reel of wire by the side of the trench." Ruth wrote back long letters describing the everyday goings-on of the family. Their simplicity comforted George.

Mallory survived World War I. "Life presents itself very much as a gift," he wrote his father from France at the end of 1918. "If I haven't escaped so many chances of death as plenty of others, still it is surprising to find myself a survivor, and it's not a lot I have always wanted. There has been so much to be said for being in the good company of the dead."

Mallory came home in 1919 and resumed teaching literature at Charterhouse. It was inevitable, after he refound his feet, that he would return to climbing. He put up new routes in Wales and Switzerland, on one ascent using the pick of his axe in a thin crack to surmount a difficulty—"dry-tooling" a half-century before the term was invented. Such virtuosity made him an obvious choice for the first two-part British Everest expedition. At thirty-four, Mallory was one of the best climbers in the world.

Mountaineering was still in its infancy in the 1920s. The tools and techniques of the craft were primitive, courage paramount. Mountaineers climbed on short lengths of weak rope without protection. Falls were frequently fatal. Little had changed since British climber Edward Whymper led his successful but ill-starred expedition to the top of the "unclimbable" Matterhorn in 1865. (Four members of Whymper's seven-man team died on the descent.) Though most of the relatively easy peaks in the Alps had been climbed by 1920—and Kilimanjaro, Aconcagua, and McKinley had been summited via their least intimidating slopes—the vast majority of the world's summits were still untested. For an alpinist, the biggest blank on the map was the Himalayas. Only a few of the range's hundreds of high mountains had been climbed, and none of its fourteen peaks over 8,000 meters had ever been seriously attempted.

Though Everest had been determined to be the highest mountain on earth in 1852 by the Survey of India, geopolitical problems had prevented close inspection for over half a century. The Tibetans called the immense massif Chomolungma, "Goddess Mother of the World." The survey had labeled it Peak XV, but in 1865, the year of Appomattox and the Matterhorn tragedy, it was officially renamed Mount Everest, in honor of Sir George Everest, the surveyor general of India.

In the aftermath of World War I, Everest was "the third Pole," the still unattained zenith of adventure in a world where the North and South Poles had at last been conquered. Sponsored by the Royal Geographic Society and the Alpine Club, the plan was for two expeditions, one in 1921 as a reconnaissance, one in 1922 to attempt an ascent. Mallory considered turning down the opportunity. By now, he had two young daughters and a five-month-old son. Everest was an enormous commitment. Both expeditions would take six months, three times longer than the average Himalayan expedition of today: two months sailing to and from, two months trekking in and out, two months on or near the mountain. Even so, Mallory and Ruth concluded that he had to go.

On the 1921 expedition, one of the four climbers died of exhaustion on the trek in, and a second, also suffering from exhaustion, was ordered back for fear of a similar end. Mallory explored, climbed minor peaks, and helped map the northern approach to Everest. The mountain, he wrote, had "the most stupendous ridges and appalling precipices that I have ever seen." In 1922, Mallory made it to 26,800 feet without oxygen and two other climbers went to 27,235 feet with oxygen, both records. But these feats came at a horrible cost: seven porters died in an avalanche and half the climbing team became severely frostbitten.

"It's an infernal mountain," Mallory wrote from base camp at the end of the second expedition, "cold and treacherous. Frankly the game is not good enough; the risks of getting caught are too great; the margin of strength when men are at great height is too small."

Back home, Mallory immediately set out on a five-month lecture tour through England and North America. He needed the money. He spoke in New York, Washington, Montreal, Philadelphia, Toledo, Buffalo, Chicago, Iowa City. Nonetheless, the trip was a financial failure. He made friends with American climbers but was exasperated by the press. One reporter, he wrote to Ruth, "wanted me to say that the great mountaineers of the expedition were all men of scientific training, or that mental training had more to do with the matter than physique. Can you imagine anything more childish? But I expect that is just what Americans are."

In March 1923, near the end of his American tour, a weary Mallory was questioned by a New York Times reporter, who, like so many others, wanted a simple answer to Why climb Everest? "Because it's there," said Mallory. And thus the most famous statement in mountaineering history was probably little more than a throwaway remark contrived for a press unwilling to take the time to listen to more complicated explanations.

In 1924, for the third time in four years, Mallory left for Everest. "How thrilled you must be to be going out again!" an admirer exclaimed. Mallory's response: "You know I am leaving my wife and children behind me."

"I don't expect to come back," he confided to Geoffrey Keynes, an old friend from Cambridge. The expedition would be "more like war than mountaineering."

He knew what was in store for him—the cold, the fatigue, the wind. So why did he go? For George Mallory it was not simply about being the first. "I have not been on these two expeditions to witness the spectacle of myself breaking a record," he said in one of his lectures. "In the whole scale of values, clearly, I think, records of this sort can't weigh in the balance against the serious work of everyday life."

Mallory's truest answer is one that is neither cryptic nor wholly explicable: climbing had become his art. Like any artist who gradually moves toward greater and greater challenges, and through this process defines himself and interprets the world around him, Mallory had reached Everest through a lifelong love of mountaineering— from the first boyhood thrills of climbing trees to the slow accretion of acumen and insight through hundreds of nights on the ground and days on snow. Mallory *deserved* to climb Everest. He could no more abandon climbing than Picasso could have abandoned painting.

"I suppose we go to Mount Everest, granted the opportunity, because—in a word—we can't help it," he told an audience in America. "Or, to state the matter rather differently, because we are mountaineers. . . . To refuse the adventure is to run the risk of drying up like a pea in its shell."

Not long after Mallory was lost on Everest, his wife wrote to a friend of the family:

"I know George did not mean to be killed; he meant not to be so hard. . . . I don't think I do feel that his death makes me the least more proud of him. It is his life that I loved and love. I know so absolutely that he could not have failed in courage or self-sacrifice. Whether he got to the top of the mountain or did not, whether he lived or died, makes no difference to my admiration of him."

Once a Phantom

Sue lifts herself onto one elbow and whispers in the dark.

"What are you doing?"

I am lying on my side staring through the veil of netting.

"What's wrong?"

"Nothing."

I roll from my side onto my back, close my eyes, and pretend to go back to sleep. Just another night camping in Kenya. Sue sighs, lies back, cuddles herself down into her sleeping bag. I pivot my head and open my eyes.

I am watching a thief.

I had been waiting for him in my sleep. When he arrived I awoke. I can do that now. Footfalls at a hundred paces and I wake up. A shadow crosses my eyelids, closed for hours, and my eyes snap open. Sometimes it's nothing so obvious. The stars in my dreams are suddenly misaligned or the moon has its mouth open and is trying to speak to me. Sue knows I can do this; it is why she can sleep. She teases me, but she doesn't mean it: she was there the night we were attacked.

She's fallen back to sleep, her forehead against my shoulder, hair across her face. I turn carefully back onto my side. The thief looks in my direction.

We were told he was here. This morning we got off the bus from Mombasa covered in heat and dust and immediately caught another one going on up the coast toward Somalia. The road wound through the bush with occasional glimpses of the Indian Ocean. Past a seaside village we saw a handmade sign for camping and shouted up to the driver. The bus slowed down and we jumped off.

The campground was just off the beach, a square plot carved from the labyrinthine thicket. Tall trees with umbrella-like canopies protected campers from the African sun. There was an outhouse, a mossy concrete shower, a concrete sink with a rusted spigot. You could hear the susurrus of the ocean. After we paid, the woman who owned the place, a lumpish expat of indeterminate origin, told us to pitch up anywhere we pleased.

"Watch y'selfs though, child'en," she added, a cigarette hanging from the corner of her mouth. "We got ourselves a thief 'ere. He don't always come 'round, but when he does folks wake up with somethin' missin'. He must be one wily midnight man, 'cause nobody's caught 'im yet."

Now, watching him through the netting, I know why: he is a ghost. He floats, never letting so much as an elbow get caught under direct moonlight, as if it were an acid that would burn him. His movement is so silent and fluid you are inclined to believe you haven't seen anything at all.

We were attacked on an ordinary night. Before you learn to recognize the clues, this is always the way it seems. We were cycling down the Adriatic Coast in a country once called Yugoslavia. Sue and I had already bicycled across Western Europe together twice. Drank cheap wine and wheeled wild through Paris at two in the morning, ground over snowy passes in the Alps, hammered into the wind along the icy North Sea. This trip, we were riding a circle through Eastern Europe—south into Yugoslavia, east across Romania, north along the Black Sea, west across Hungary.

It was a quiet summer evening. Down the beach there was a group of drunk men shouting and laughing. Relaxed after a hundred-mile day, we watched the sun sink into a Maxfield Parrish sea. When it was dark we wheeled our bicycles off the beach into the forest. We couldn't see a thing but it didn't matter, we had our system dialed and the tent was up in minutes. We locked the bikes, crawled inside, zipped up, and fell fast asleep, innocently unwary for the last time in our lives.

I knew the thief would come tonight. Not long after we set up camp, a crowd arrived: twenty young, nubile Europeans driving London-to-Capetown in a gigantic, all-terrain truck with axles four feet off the ground. They spread out immediately, tan and half-nude, stringing clotheslines, playing radios, setting all their coveted accoutrements right out in the open. How could he resist.

And yet he didn't appear until three A.M. He waited, perhaps just outside the clearing, hidden in the bush, watching, eyes like a cat's. Perhaps down the road in a bar drinking warm Fanta. Either way, he was calm and patient, like all successful thieves. He waited until everyone was so deeply asleep he could hear it—that slow sonorous breathing rising from the tents like mist.

Then he slipped into our midst and my eyes clicked open. He went directly to the closest tent. His slight, ephemeral shape disappeared instantly, as if melting into the nylon. In moments he reappeared and slid back into the thicket behind the tent. He was so soundless it was as if I were watching him through glass.

I could have yelled and shot out of the tent, racing for him through the aluminum light, but then he would simply have vanished. No doubt he has a dozen escape routes unknown to all but him, who designed them in full daylight, the other villagers assuming the muted cracking was just a boy gathering firewood.

Minutes passed, then I spotted him again as he entered a second tent, not from the front but from behind. It was like a magic trick. He was crouched at the back, then gone. That he was inside the tent and they were still asleep shocked me. Perhaps his breath, like a leopard's, hypnotized them. Perhaps he whispered words that sank into their dreams and beguiled them. Again I debated taking chase but decided the time was still not right. The tent was too close to his exit; he would still escape.

When he reemerged from the second tent and carried his plunder into the bush, I thought, That's it. He will not return. He's too smart. Enough risk for one night. He'll walk back to his hut on the beach, hide his new possessions in a hole in the floor, and slip into bed beside his wife.

But he came back and my heart leapt. Sweet greed, the Achilles' heel of the deft-fingered and fleet-footed. On his third sortie he slipped all the way into the middle of camp, then froze. This is when Sue woke. She must have felt something; she too has learned to mistrust the safety of sleep. But then when she asked what was wrong, I lied, and she went back to sleep, leaving me to watch for whatever was out there.

We learn how to sleep in the safety of our mothers' wombs, then in the safety of our parents' arms, then in the safety of our families' homes. Once you have been attacked in your sleep, this naive sense of security is shattered. Sleep is never the same again. There are times I lie awake and listen so hard I can't separate what is a harbinger from what is nothing at all. Then the danger passes. I am still trying to learn how to make the distinction. There are so many close calls we sleep right through.

This is what few will admit: to travel is to become a target. To travel is to purposefully make yourself vulnerable, to throw yourself into the world like a boy leaps into a lake. This is why so many good things happen. The widow you've never met taking you in as the son she lost fifty years before. The blind child who guides you by the hand out to the man who bakes bread. The night it rained while the stars shone. The day it snowed while the sun shone.

This is also why bad things happen.

If you travel enough, something bad will happen to you. This is not a probability, this is a certainty. To desperate people, hurt people, helpless people—the world is full of these—you are an opportunity, not an individual. You are who they are waiting for. The moment you arrive their plan goes into effect. If you are lucky you will lose nothing that can't be easily replaced: a wallet, a camera, a car. These are not things to mourn. Go home, go back to work, replace them, be thankful. If you are unlucky, however, you will be hurt. The bruises and cuts and the bones will heal, but you will be changed forever.

The thief has been standing perfectly motionless for over an hour now. He has been there so long my mind is trying to make me believe he is not there—that the dark stain beside the tree is just part of the tree. But I know better. This is his special skill: to become invisible. I imagine he learned it young. Something coveted quick into the pocket in the marketplace at dusk. So easy. A few years later he is the only boy in the village with basketball shoes. Only boy with a tape recorder. He never gets caught. He is a prestidigitator. In his heart he doesn't understand why everyone is not a thief.

But why has he stopped? No one in the campground has stirred or spoken, save the occasional half-sentence burbled up from the depths of slumber. Could he somehow have heard Sue's whispers? No.

Perhaps.

Yes, of course—he must have heard. His ears have adapted to his trade just like the rest of him. Ears of a fox, stealth of a coyote. If he heard her question, he heard my answer, and he knows I was lying. If he knows this, he knows I am watching him now. But what tent am I in? There are more than a dozen. It is obvious. The small tent with its back against the wall, like where a man sits in a bar after he's been in too many fights. The one positioned at such an angle that someone inside can survey the entire campground.

Perhaps he is beginning to have second thoughts. Perhaps now he wishes he had not come so deep into the campground but had gathered up his loot and the night's good fortune and left.

Lying on my side I stare at him across the moonlit ground and know he is staring at me. My stomach begins to thump. I realize I have already made a mistake. This is the way with mistakes. They are already done when you finally notice them. My arms are down at my sides but the knife is somewhere above my head in the corner of the tent. I have made this mistake before.

In Yugoslavia.

I woke in the middle of the night. I'd heard something. I strained, lifting my head off the ground and holding myself in that position. Eventually I decided it was just branches in the wind. It didn't *feel* like just branches in the wind, but I assessed the situation logically. The tent was well hidden, the night was half over, we were just two bicyclists for God's sakes.

From childhood we are taught to be rational. To control our emotions. We learn the scientific method as if it were the Eleventh Commandment. This is a mistake. Some things are not identifiable, but they are real. They mean something and they should not be discounted.

The thief does not know of my mistake. He knows that I have been awake, that I have been watching him. And though he is watching me watch him, he cannot see me. I am inside my tent behind the shroud of netting. If he suddenly fled, from where I am I could not catch him before he disappeared into his escape tunnels. So why doesn't he simply run?

He knows I do not have a gun because I have not made a move.

With a gun you are reckless. With a gun I would rush out and with the help of the moonlight perhaps wing him before he made it back to the honeycombed bush.

I must have a knife. He knows I have a knife, otherwise I would not be so arrogant as to stare at him. If I did not have a weapon I would have shouted by now.

But I don't believe he has a gun either. A man with a gun does not move like he does. He doesn't need to. If he had a gun he would not be lithesome, flitting like a phantom through the night. He has a knife. He entered the second tent from the end where there is no entrance. I do not know what kind of knife, nothing big, something small and sharp.

The moon has moved but he remains in the safety of shade. He is standing more still than a man can stand. He has become wood after all, part of the tree. Perhaps he is waiting for me to fall back to sleep. But he must know better. If I have waited this long I can wait all night. All week. A man can wait years for revenge.

Why does he not test me? There are so many tents, so many victims. Why does he not continue his raid?

Perhaps it isn't greed after all. I realize I have underestimated him. It is no longer about the mastercraft of thievery. It has become personal. It's about us. We are each waiting for the other to make the first move. We are each waiting for an opening.

My eyes are wide open but they are tired. I let them blink. When they come open he is moving toward me, circling, staying in the shadows. By this act he has underestimated me. We have taken the time to get to know each other and now he believes he knows me. Knows how I will react, what I will do. This is a common mistake humans make with each other.

He is closing in, skimming, staying low, almost crouching, moving like a predator. He is coming closer, quickly closer, when suddenly the attack in Yugoslavia convulses through me like electricity . . .

something in my dreams I can't make out something I can't recognize but should but it's too late. A purplewhite explosion in my head and an instant awareness of attackers all around us and I'm throwing myself over Sue like a table and there is screaming but it is not coming from her because Sue is as still as a dead child. I am not feeling the blows not the first boot to the side of my head not the kicks or the punches or the blood because my hands are desperately scrambling for my knife in the blackness over the tent floor. A silver blade comes down through the top of the tent splitting it open like a wound but I have found the knife and am on my feet stabbing twirling slashing but now they are spreading away into the darkness and I'm flying after them through tunnels. The screaming stops. I realize the horrific screeching has been coming from my mouth. I run back to Sue. She is numbly gathering up the remains of our possessions in the forest, not crying, not even shaking . . .

The thief is right beside the tent. I am waiting for him. I haven't moved and by this act I have informed him. He is turning to run but I am already bolting out scooping up the knife, racing not for him but where he will run to escape. He didn't expect this. It confuses him. I'm yelling "Thief! Thief!" and campers are turning on their flashlights and stepping out of their tents. He can't go where he was planning to go and trips on a guy line and falls to his knees. He knows tents have guy lines, snares, but he has never tripped before. He is bewildered. He has lost his grace, his nimbleness, his invisibility. He is back on his feet, running now through the moonlight and it is all over him as if it were burning him and he is writhing and dodges a man and tries to leap another guy line but it catches his leg and then two European men are on him like hyenas pulling down a gazelle and he looks up at me.

It's over. I go back to the tent. Sue is standing in the moonlight with a sleeping bag wrapped around her shoulders. She puts her hand in mine and feels it shaking.

It will be dawn soon. We go for a walk along the beach and watch the water and the sky slowly gather light and turn colors. As the moon silently disappears the sun rises out of the flaming Indian Ocean.

We walk back to the campground. They have bound the thief to the side of the all-terrain truck with a heavy rope. He must stand on his tiptoes not to strangle. His body is twisted with his hands tied behind his back. His T-shirt and trousers are soaked with his own blood. Blood is oozing from his mouth and eyes and crusted black in his ears. The local villagers are torturing him. Children are stabbing him in the genitals with sticks. The older boys are taking turns punching his head. Old women are spitting on him.

Sue drops my hand, runs forward, grabs the stick from one of the children and steps in front of the thief. The crowd stares at her, unimpressed with her outrage. If word got out, this one thief could ruin the lost hippie tourist trade and these villagers would lose their livelihood. With no one to buy fruit or shell necklaces or leather sandals, their millennium of poverty would instantly return.

Or perhaps this is just more rationalization. Perhaps they are simply being cruel. We humans have an almost limitless capacity for evil.

Sue shouts at them to go away, but her voice cracks. She wipes her cheeks with the back of her hand.

"You're sick!" she yells. "You're all sick." She is pointing the stick at the crowd, and they back up, but they don't leave. They wait, like vultures.

Crime and punishment can be disproportionate. This is a world without clear boundaries. Sometimes we are predators, sometimes prey, sometimes both.

In the evening the police finally come. They cut him down and beat him with their black clubs on the bottoms of his feet so he will never again be a phantom.

Thin Ice

Halfway up Ben Nevis, splayed against hollow ice like a cat clinging to a curtain blown out the window of a skyscraper, I realize that falling is out of the question. It's always good to get that worry out of the way.

The mountain hurls down another waterfall of spindrift and I duck my head. Wet and heavy as a stream of concrete, the cascade pours over my helmet and shoulders. I hunch in against the face. It has been raining ceaselessly since the day we arrived in Scotland. The rain is rapidly deteriorating the ice, causing it to randomly collapse. The snow passes around me, slides over a bulge of ice below my feet, and disappears into the clouds.

I resume climbing, sinking the axes in above my head. When I pull up, both picks begin to shear through the ice. It's unnerving. I step up with alacrity, kicking my crampons in with too much force. My boots plunge through the veneer of ice into sugary, bottomless snow. I am barely attached to the wall. Above me is nothing but plates of gray ice pretending they are affixed to the rock when I know damn well they're merely suspended on vertical pillows of powder. Down between my feet, the ropes drop into swirling, sepulchral oblivion. I lift out one axe, twirl it, slam in the adze, and gingerly test it. It appears to hold and I continue upward. One of the absurd little secrets to reaching the top of something is simply to get yourself so far out that retreat is more horrifying than carrying on.

I remind myself that I can never be off balance. The sick, glorious sport of ice climbing depends on physical equipoise, which depends on mental tranquillity, which in turn depends on a blend of faith and self-confidence as smooth as single-malt Scotch. I must slow down. I must direct one limb at a time as if I were a dancer deliberately prolonging each movement. That way, if an axe or foothold should fail, I will still be tenuously fastened to the ice at three other points.

I place screws in the honeycombed ice as I ascend, although I know they could not hold a fall. The ice is too rotten. I recall with nauseating terror that this route was originally climbed with just one ice axe and no protection. My droop-picked, shark-toothed tools hook into the ice like claws, but the sole ice axe of the first ascensionist had a straight, ninety-degree pick with tiny teeth. You couldn't sink it into steep ice and hang on for dear life—the pick would pop right out. Instead, the climber used the wood-shafted ice axe as precisely that—an axe, hacking out a handhold above his head with the adze, grasping the hold and pulling up on it with one woolly-mittened hand, chopping another pigeonhole, swapping the leashless axe to the opposite hand, and doing another pull-up. Handholds became footholds, although the deeper and more sound you made them, the more exhausted you became. Hence early masters cut tiny, ephemeral steps. It seems insane, bold beyond believability. And yet I know that this route, the chute, is just one of dozens put up in Scotland in the 1950s and 1960s by a genius named Jimmy Marshall.

I climb until the ropes go taut, bury both tools, and begin brushing the snow off the walls of rock around me. I'm praying for a crack in which to place protection—knife blade, stopper, chock, cam, anything. But the stone is monolithic. I twist two screws into a smear of ice, sling them, sling my ice tools, equal-tension it all together with one knot, and let go a big fat lie: "On belay!"

Dave Getchel and Geoff Heath, my American partners, will simul-climb, one on each rope. Getch is a squirt of a man, far stronger than his ribby physique would suggest. An unregenerate Mainer, he learned to climb New England glace with his father a quarter-century ago. Getch can flawlessly duplicate the Scotsman's brogue. Geoff is a stolid, solid Montana engineer who has been an ice climber since the 1970s, when the sport first became popular in the United States.

I suck up the rope, stare out into the vertiginous maelstrom, and keep my ears peeled for signals. I'm still grappling with the thought of climbing this face with only one ice axe. The perilousness of it all. The naked insecurity. An uncanny sense of dread begins to well up inside me. Suddenly I catch the wisp of a distant scream. Assuming one of my compadres has slipped, I brace for the fall, a routine reflex; however, because I do not believe the anchors will hold, my heart plugs my throat and I wait to be plucked into eternity.

But no weight yanks on the ropes. I don't understand. When Getch and Geoff reach the belay I ask if either of them screamed. They shake their heads.

I begin to question myself. Perhaps my ticklish perch and black thoughts inspired fear to fabricate the howl, just as a young child left alone in the dark will hear evil voices.

It's Geoff's lead. He examines the dubious belay anchors. "Guess I won't fall."

"Welcome to Scotland, laddie," growls Getch in his best, through-the-beard burr.

Geoff disappears up into sleet, leading with speed, precision, and no ascertainable doubt. When he brings us up we discover he has placed only three screws in 200 feet, but his belay is reassuringly good, a long sling around a big boulder. Getch takes the gear and leads on while I get out the monocular and scan the couloir, Coire Na Ciste, a thousand feet below. In the interstices between spinning updrafts and curling mist, I spot something. Perhaps it is only a ridge of rock poking out high in the snow-choked cwm. I study it until I'm sure.

"Geoff."

We are standing side by side on the two-inch ledge of ice. I hold the monocular against his eye so his hands can continue to belay. He tilts his head, peers through the spyglass for a full minute, then nods, turns away, and refocuses on Getch climbing silently high above us.

The rock outcrop is the body of a man, lying face down on the steep cirque, arms folded under his head as if he were napping.

"Remember," says Hamish MacInnes, seventy, reminiscing about the 1950s, "at this time the ice axe was still considered a cutting implement, not a tool for direct adhesion. One had to be completely ambidextrous. Hang on by one hand and cut with the other. You got into the habit of being much further out than climbers are today."

MacInnes leans forward, the blade of his nose protruding from a sallow, stern face. "It was strenuous and bloody dangerous."

Getch and I have cornered MacInnes in the pub of the Ballachulish Hotel in the bleak feudal valley of Glencoe, Scotland. It is still pouring outside, great swaths of black liquid. The relentlessness of the rain seems almost malevolent. Already I am beginning to believe that every Scot with any sense left this soggy land the minute Australia was discovered. There is good reason why those who stayed, drink.

But Hamish MacInnes, with a thin white beard and yet still big-shouldered, reminding you of the force he once was, has ordered orange juice. MacInnes is a climbing legend, one of the few who put up new routes over several decades and somehow survived the bad gear and worse weather. MacInnes estimates he has lost forty friends to the mountains. He, along with Graeme Nicol and the lyric mountain churl Tom Patey (who died in 1970 falling off a sea stack called the Maiden) did the first ascent of Ben Nevis's Zero Gully in 1957, then one of the hardest ice climbs in the world.

"I climbed a lot with Patey," MacInnes says. "He was always rather amusing. One day he came down to see me with a couple of those hand cultivators that the ladies use in the garden. He figured you could strap the claws to your hands." MacInnes allows himself a thin-lipped grin.

"Unfortunately these claws needed some means of forcing them into the ice. Patey wasn't much of an engineer."

But MacInnes was. He had been designing mountaineering equipment since the late 1940s. His own homemade, heavy-headed, incline-picked ice hammer had been nicknamed the Message by fellow mountaineers. The mythic Message, like the sword in the stone, had an all-metal shaft, an innovation MacInnes believes was his greatest contribution to climbing.

"It was quite common to find broken axes in rescues," he continues. "Three people died while attempting Zero Gully because of wood-shafted axes. They were using the axes in a traditional boot-axe belay, and when one of them fell, the rope snapped the axe heads right off. We found the wood stumps still stuck in the snow."

MacInnes designed the first all-metal ice axe in 1948, began mass production in 1960, and by the mid-1970s had perfected his notorious, prehistoric-looking Terrordactyl ice hammer.

"The inclined pick and the metal shaft, those are what really started the ice climbing revolution," MacInnes says.

I try to get him to talk more about the glory days, but he is disinclined to do so.

"You know who you should talk to? That Yank. Yvon Chouinard."

When we step from the Ballachulish, it's still raining. Big black pellets. "Ach, this bloody rain," groans MacInnes, "you never really get used to it."

Yvon Chouinard went to the Alps in the summer of 1966 to test ice axes. When the twenty-eight-year-old gear maker–cum–climbing bum returned to California, he stepped back up to his anvil and started experimenting.

"I would take my own axe and reforge it," he says. "Different pick angles, different tooth configurations, different adzes."

We're sitting at the kitchen table in Ron Kauk's cabin in El Portal, California, a stone's throw from Yosemite, Chouinard's spiritual homeland.

"I've never been an inventor. I would start from existing ideas or existing products." Chouinard's speech is as compact and powerful as his small body. It was through working as a blacksmith that he forged his ideas. His 1978 book, Climbing Ice, is the literary foundation of modern ice climbing.

"It took me eight years to write that damn book. I had to travel all over the world and study the different ice climbing techniques."

Mountaineering was the mother of ice climbing. A century ago, mountains were climbed in hobnailed boots with stafflike ice axes, footsteps laboriously cut all the way to the top. Snow was preferred, ice avoided. Then came crampons, largely eliminating the need for chopping steps. Climbing mountains became faster, and more difficult routes soon went up. By the end of the 1940s, most of the great steep faces of the Alps, from the Eiger to the Matterhorn, had been climbed. Yet throughout the 1950s and 1960s, climbing pure ice, without a mountain, was the obscure passion of the mad Scots and a handful of continental climbers. This changed for good when, in 1970, Chouinard and climbing buddy Doug Tompkins (who had co-founded the North Face four years earlier) showed up in Scotland with radical hand-forged tools. They had curved picks that mimicked the arc of the swing of a carpenter's hammer—or perhaps the arc of the swing of a blacksmith. They also had deep teeth that crocodiled all the way up the beak of the pick. Such picks stuck easily in Scottish ice, and in a single evolutionary swing changed the nascent sport of ice climbing forever: no more chopping handholds.

As Rob Collister wrote in Mountain magazine, "The development of the curved pick for axes and hammers was an event in ice climbing history comparable to the introduction of crampons in the 1890s, or the use of front-points and ice pitons in the thirties. It could prove more revolutionary than either, since it makes for both greater speed and greater security."

Chouinard put this quote in his book, but true to his crusty, contrarian nature, the founder of Patagonia seems dismayed, even disappointed, at the monster he created.

"Front-pointing with two modern tools just has no elegance," he argues. "It completely eliminates the need for technique. Those tools made ice climbing democratic." He snorts with disgust. "Now anybody can climb vertical ice. I don't care if I ever climb vertical ice again. For me it's so boring. Your grandmother could climb vertical ice on her first day out, the tools are so efficient."

I can't say I agree. That would have to be one wild, kickass grandmother.

Chouinard claims he is a Luddite, but this is not possible. Luddites are not designers of revolutionary tools, whether they be silicon chips or ice axes; Luddites embrace the technological status quo. Chouinard has made a life of fighting the status quo. Antithetically, Chouinard devoted a substantial portion of his book to one-tool climbing.

"Climbing with one tool," he says, "you always have to end up in balance, because if you're not, you're fucked. I really love that whole idea of finding ways to balance yourself. You have to be a real genius to pull it off. You know who was the all-time master of that stuff? Jimmy Marshall."

It's raining in Edinburgh, the city's Gothic spire to Robert Louis Stevenson shrouded in dark clouds, as Getch and I search the slippery streets. We find Jimmy Marshall's home on a narrow cobblestone lane, and knock.

"Come in, come in!"

We are escorted up steep stairs to a spacious, book-lined living room. Our host offers tea. Marshall, seventy-one, is a spry, slender man with the gayest of eyes. He radiates an ineluctable lightness of being. He has been an architect his whole life. Getch and I pepper him with questions about the famous routes he put up, but he is loath to dwell on his accomplishments. Instead he relates anecdotes of the "tremendous ice climbers" of Scotland who came before him:

Norman Collie, who in 1894 made the first winter ascent of Tower Ridge on Ben Nevis in 1894. A man who realized after just one climb that "mountain climbing became more important to me than fishing."

John MacKenzie, Collie's partner for fifty years, who would strip off his boots and climb in his woolen socks to gain more friction—a technique Marshall admits to having resorted to himself.

Harold Raeburn, who did the first ascent of Green Gully on Ben Nevis in 1909, a route that would not be repeated for thirty-one years. A man who wrote only one book, Mountaineering Art, but wrote it powerfully: "The mountains, like the oceans, have always been the home of the marvelous and the terrible from the earliest dawn of history. Man, in the main, was and still is, an inhabitant of the flat, and fat, places of the earth."

Bill Murray, who wrote the first draft of his classic history, Mountaineering in Scotland, on toilet paper as a prisoner of war in Bavaria during World War II, only to have it discovered and confiscated by the Gestapo. And then wrote the whole thing again, from memory, in a prison camp in Czechoslovakia.

"Murray inspired a lot of young people to take up ice climbing," Marshall tells us, his eyes gleaming. "I was walking the Highlands a lot in the 1940s. We were climbing in snow and ice just as a natural sort of thing. That's what you did. It's so damned attractive in the hills in winter, you know. Winter's a classic time. It's absolutely wonderful.

"It's really all about linking with nature. Coming close to rocks and hills and exposing yourself to wilderness and wild weather and all the rest of it. It gives you a tremendous sense of belonging, of being part of it. The poetry of it." Marshall pauses and looks out the window longingly, as if he could see the Scottish Highlands from Edinburgh. "It's quite overwhelming."

Getch tells Marshall of our trembling ascent of the Chute and how weevily and variable the ice seemed to be.

"That's the great joy of winter climbing, isn't it?" he says. "I mean, there's really no such thing as a first ascent!"

We ask about the climbing techniques Marshall employed to climb bad ice with one bad tool.

"We had this terrible labor of hacking away at the ice," Marshall replies with a rueful snicker. "A hell of a job it was. And then the knack of going over a final end of a pitch, you were just walking in wee scrapes in the thinner surfaces. It was quite hairy."

Marshall suddenly springs from his chair as if he were half a century younger, disappears from the room for a moment, and returns with his wood-shafted ice axe—an aesthetic antique with the tiny teeth on the straight pick almost worn away and the edges of the adze completely rounded off from chopping hundreds of thousands of holds.

He stands in the living room and gives us a demonstration, nimbly dancing up an invisible wall of ice. Raising the axe above his head to chop handholds, two precise blows for each one, spreading his legs, leaning delicately from one side to the other, stepping up, throwing the ice axe to his other hand, and chopping another set of tiny holds.

"The real skill was being able to balance and cut steps. Can you imagine it!"

His movements are so exact, so graceful, Getch and I are speechless.

"With the stick-and-pick techniques of modern tools, you're not actually in balance. You don't need to be because you're just always supported by your tools and your crampons."

Like a mime, he makes another clean, purposeful step up.

"It seems desperate," I say.

"We didn't think it was particularly risky," Marshall responds, still deftly clinging to his imaginary wall.

"Did you ever fall?" I ask.

He stops, lowers his old axe, and drops his lively eyes to the two boys on his couch.

"I have never fallen. That really was virtually death."

We were coming down from the Chute when the apocalyptic, death-collecting *wump-wump-wump* of a military helicopter stormed up the Allt a' Mhuilinn valley. While the chopper hovered above Coire Na Ciste, bouncing violently in the downdrafts, we looked on as the body was hooked to a cable by rescuers and reeled up into the aircraft.

We got the story in the Ben Nevis pub that night while the rain ran in veins down the smoky windowpanes. Apparently the poor kid was only eighteen years old. He had the guidebook and could name off all the routes. And he had shiny new high-tech ice gear. What he did not have was experience—years spent in the mountains learning about himself and his connection to rock and snow and ice.

He decided to solo Green Gully and did fine until the last few feet of the climb. Coming over the cornice at the very top, he inexplicably put his knees onto the ice and slipped off backward. Just lost his balance.

MOUNTAINS

Somebody Else's Rum

It had been pouring for days. Along the coast we tromped through walls of dark rain. At timberline we clambered up through swaths of sleet. On the glacier we pushed into whiteouts of confetti. It's what we'd been told to expect. We kept our heads down and our hoods up and water skimmed off our noses.

One evening the weather momentarily broke. We'd pitched our tent in the vastness of the Franklin Glacier and were brewing tea when the hands of the sky began tearing the clouds apart. Just as the light began to fade, we saw the mountain for the first time. It emerged from the mist like a sinister castle: jagged black ridges and deeply crevassed glaciers swooping up to a stone tower plated with snow. The summit was a horned menace sheathed in ice. We passed the monocular back and forth in silence.

I pulled out my copy of the 1934 *Canadian Alpine Journal* and read out loud: "An incredible nightmarish thing that must be seen to be believed."

John Harlin, my partner, squinted through the spyglass and nodded gravely.

We'd been pumping ourselves up for this mountain for two months. Its magnetism had sucked us in like metal filings. Tempests that dumped ten feet of snow in one night, octopusal glaciers, an unknown, unclimbed wall—the more treacherous the tale the more inspired we became. Which is the way it always is when you've spent too much time indoors.

Every year for the past seven, John and I had promised each other we'd do an expedition together—and every year something got in the way. Financial worries, wives or kids, misguided goals, bad schedules. Adulthood is an insidious process of accretion. If you're not vigilant, you begin to grow a shell, a carapace that you are expected to carry lightly: the rigid, high-stress hull of security, status, status quo. The thicker the better, right up until it crushes you. On the inside, whether you can still feel it or not, your soul is trying to claw its way out.

I was beginning to fear for John, and lately, for myself. The integument of everyday life seemed to have begun to harden. We were both working too much. John was struggling to keep a small magazine alive; I was battling to finish a book that had lost its bearings. We'd call each other at midnight, still in our offices—appalling for a couple of climbing bums who once lived out of a VW van and survived on tins of sardines. John, in particular, was in trouble. He'd spent so much time trying to build a business he was in danger of becoming one more Cubicle Man, ass-wedged between a green screen and four white walls.

Late one night, John started whispering darkly about how much he'd given up, how he'd "sacrified years."

It was time to escape.

I'd been studying the climbing history of one of Canada's most mythical mountains: Waddington. At 13,186 feet, it's the highest peak in the Coast Range of British Columbia, and has a splendidly nasty reputation. It is remote and rarely climbed. Storms last two or three or even four weeks. After reading every account of every expedition that had been to the mountain, I'd discovered a secret: the south face was still unclimbed.

To make sure I called Don Serl, veteran of over thirty expeditions into the Coast Range, at his home in Vancouver. He laughed at my dilettantism. "That's the route Wiessner and House used on the first ascent in 1936," he said.

Fritz Wiessner, a grizzled, square-headed German expatriate, and

William Pendleton House, a lanky Yale alum, were legendary early hardmen. (In 1937 they made the first ascent of Devils Tower together.) Their route up Waddington had been repeated few times in the last half-century.

I told Serl that I had reviewed the topographic maps and that it looked like Wiessner and House had actually climbed the west face, not the south face.

Serl went silent.

"There was a man named Alec Dalgleish who died trying the south face in 1934," I said. "He slipped and the rope sliced and he fell a thousand feet, but . . . I think the south face is still a virgin."

Serl knew I'd done my homework. He became cagey. "Well, you'll just have to find out for yourself," he said. The fact that he wouldn't discuss the matter further was a dead giveaway. The true south face of Waddington was unclimbed, and he knew it. He just didn't want some cowboys riding in and rustling it from the Canadians.

I e-mailed John: "This is it. You and me. Waddington. New route. May."

John wrote back immediately, excited, desirous of details but still stuck on work, family, his busy life. I left the same message on his phone machine: "You and me. Waddington. New route. May."

The bush plane bounced through dark clouds and hooked around knots of lightning before belly-flopping into an abandoned logging camp at the head of Knight Inlet. We jumped out, dragged off our packs, and stood there in the rain while the pilot spun 180 and skipped off into the clouds.

The minute John had said yes, he'd upped the ante: "One condition: we do it the hard way—from the ocean." This was typical John Harlin. As far as we could discover, no one had climbed Waddington after marching in from the sea in years—perhaps decades.

Our plans were adolescent in their simplicity: walk up an old log-ging road, climb onto the glacier, and ski to the mountain, a thirty-mile trip we figured would take three days. We'd hiked less than a mile before our plan fell apart.

One of the many problems with the indoor life is you start to think that all the secondhand cyberinfo you're gathering has some validity. Don't kid yourself. Empiricism is the path to knowledge, or at least a life.

Our maps claimed there was a logging road. There was no log-ging road. Of course there was no logging road. This valley had been logged a generation ago and it had been raining ever since. Alders thick as dog hair had rethatched the geography. With each step the skis strapped to our packs snagged on limbs and our feet disappeared in mud.

Another problem with living indoors is that it turns you soft as butter. Going from sea to summit meant we had to pack everything from sneakers to skis, plus twice the usual allotment of food and fuel. Our packs weighed a hundred pounds before they became drenched. Wobbling into the rain forest, we looked like a couple of old bow-legged dogs shouldering their doghouses.

We took the first game trail going our way. That it was obviously a bear trail didn't bother us until we came across a large steaming pile of poop. Thereafter we peeked around every bush. Soon enough, there he was, squatting on the trail, very large and black. We stared at him and he stared at us. Then he rolled his huge head and popped his jaw and we unfastened our hip belts and eyed the trees. Satisfied that we now knew whose kingdom we were trespassing through, he lum-bered away.

That was day one. We'd managed five miles.

Day two. More thrashing and cursing.

Day three. More thrashing and cursing until we were forced to ford the Franklin River to gain the Franklin Glacier. We searched for

the broadest, shallowest, least ferocious sweep of bone-numbing glacier water. After we found a suitable 100-yard-wide spot, John
stripped and plunged into the hip-high water, involuntarily gasping,
while I belayed from shore. Once across, he roped me over. Our toes
and legs and nuts having lost consciousness, we stumbled around col-
lecting driftwood, built a proper Boy Scout bonfire (one cup stove
fuel, two cups pack trash, one cord wood) and proceeded to roast
ourselves back to life.

When blood returned to our limbs we made camp, then curled
up around the campfire as naturally as our distant forebears.

"Mark, you feel it?" In the firelight, John's eyes gleamed like a
wolf's.

Something was happening to us. It was what we'd come for. We
were being immersed back into the physical life. It was almost as if all
the rain, the frigid river, the wilderness itself were an acid dissolving
the shell of urban existence.

I threw back my head and howled.

What all grubby anthropologists worth their weight in bones
already know, and what too many urban philosophers haven't figured
out, is that humans evolved as hardy outdoor animals. Two million
years of running naked across the veld hardwired us for life in the
wilderness. Confine humans in a cage, physical or psychological, and
like every other creature on this good earth, we become flaccid,
febrile, and feckless.

The next morning we climbed into the mouth of the Franklin
Glacier. Before us lay tilted ramps of blue ice loaded with gargantuan
boulders teetering at the angle of repose. We moved as swiftly as
possible, weaving up through perilous seracs and around towering
tombstones. We heard explosions behind us and in front of us—
apartment-size blocks of rock or ice tumbling down the glacier—
but kept moving, each step made quickly yet delicately for fear of
setting off a slide. We stayed well apart. There was no point in rop-

ing up. If something happened we could not help each other. It took us two hours to race through the icefall. On the other side we threw up the tent and camped.

That icefall was the Rubicon. We had passed into the heart of the mountains. We were starting to trust our instincts again, to believe our bodies would do what we willed them to do.

For the next two days we skied and climbed through one icefall after another, carefully picking our routes. We were quietly exultant. We laughed easily. The wild man that lurks within every human was beginning to stretch. Hibernation was over. Our faces refurred, our bodies smelled of sweat, and anything, no matter how mad, began to seem possible. When the clouds briefly parted and we got our first glimpse of the mountain, we girded ourselves in our dreams and woke ready.

On the afternoon of the sixth day we axed out a platform at the base of what we were now calling the Dalgleish Face. We needed and expected several more days of bad weather to rest up, but we set the alarm for two. We planned to pop our heads out, confirm it was still snowing, go back to sleep.

But there were stars! A blazing black-blue skyful. We fired up the stove, swilled hot chocolate, and were cramponing up the unknown, moonlit face by four. We had already agreed that I would lead the ice, John the rock. Using headlamps, we tiptoed over a thin, airy snow-bridge, shot up to a small hollow below a buttress, danced around two more barely visible crevasses, and then moved diagonally up into a steep, twisting couloir.

The snow was high-angle but of perfect consistency—the kind climbers call Styrofoam. Each swing with an axe and kick with a crampon gave an audible, reassuring thud. There were occasional bands of ice, but they were short and fun, and several hidden crevasses that sent a shot of adrenaline through me when a foot plunged into space. Once John was hit by a spindrift avalanche funneling down the couloir that almost yanked him off the face, but he recovered, choking and spitting. We rapidly simul-climbed the first 2,000 feet.

For the final 1,000 feet, the couloir narrowed and steepened into a series of ice steps and mixed climbing. It was not particularly technical, but speed was critical. Both of us felt the tug of hope and passion as if there was already a rope above, pulling us up. I placed one ice screw at the base of each section of ice, then climbed—stemming and reaching with my metal claws—without putting in more protection until I'd run out all the rope. Pitch after pitch disappeared below our feet.

John and I topped out on the south face of Mount Waddington, the Dalgleish Face, at two in the afternoon, flush with triumph, shouting into the wind—but the summit, a 1,000-foot blade of black rock, still loomed above us. The weather had turned again. It was snowing and blowing. Without stopping for food or water, we set off up the shoulder of snow toward the tower.

We were kicking steps and swinging tools when we heard it, felt it— a deep, stomach-shuddering thunder. My first thought was: it's all over. The glacier is calving and we will be pulled from the face and torn limb from limb in the tumbling ice.

But the snow beneath our crampons wasn't moving. We searched for the collapsing glacier. Nothing. John and I spun about, saw it, and instinctively hunched against the mountain.

A plane, a massive four-prop bomber, was diving straight at us. It was incomprehensible: two tiny men clinging to the side of a mountain in the middle of nowhere with a World War II kamikaze thundering in. The bomber was so vast the wings seemed to darken the sky. At the last possible moment, it pulled up and arced away. Mute with disbelief, we watched the plane rumble out toward the horizon, its size and sound diminishing. Then it hooked back.

In seconds it was bearing down on us again. It made no sense. Maybe somewhere in these remote mountains we had slipped through a crack in time. Maybe this was Austria, 1944. Maybe the glacier had calved and we were both already dead and just having one last crazy dream.

The plane was seconds from slamming into us when it reared up and we were staring at its belly and the hatch was open and a bomb was dropping out. Trailing a red streamer, the payload slammed into the bergshrund just above our heads and . . . nothing. No flash, no explosion.

The plane disappeared. Even its thunder vanished, as if the bomber had been sucked into a cosmic hole.

What could we do? We climbed up to the bomb. It was buried in the snow. John pulled on the red streamer and out came a plastic cylinder the size of a fire extinguisher.

"Bubble wrap?" John was incredulous.

"Well, open it!"

John tore at it with his ice axe and plucked out a bottle of Captain Morgan's rum. Wrapped snugly around the bottle was a magazine—Penthouse, "Special Edition: Girls of the World"—with a note: "To Jim and the boys. Good luck!"

Jim? The boys? Who cared? With a 3,000-foot drop beneath us, we cracked open the bottle, ogled the pictures, and whooped it up.

Eventually we peered back up at our mountain. It was three-thirty. Our original turnaround time had been three.

John took one last slug and grinned like the pirate on the label.

"How 'bout five."

"Five it is."

He handed me the bottle and started climbing.

It meant we might have to bivouac high on the face. We had no tent, no sleeping bag, no bivouac sack. If necessary, we'd hack a hole in the wall, rope ourselves in, hope we were still functional when the sun came up.

John took two falls trying to gain the tower from the fragile bergshrund. He was scared, but when he finally got onto the rock, he climbed as if he weren't. Such is the sangfroid that only comes with putting yourself up against something you're not sure you can do. It was steep and technical, every move had to be definitive. Slowly, hammering in too few pitons, he ran out a rope-length. He brought me up and then ran out another hundred feet, stopping in an exposed notch.

I put up the next pitch, moving as fast as possible through an ice-rimed overhang. Then he led a pitch, ice axes flashing in the evening whirl of sun and snow. Then I led a pitch.

Then it was five. The sun was sinking, the wind screeching, the temperature dropping like a shotgunned sparrow, and the summit was still above us. We would soon be benighted.

Much is made of turnaround times in mountaineering. People die when they break the rules. People die when they go too far. It's all true, but it's only half the story. No maxim applies to every situation. Only fools and cowards follow every rule.

And you have to know your limits. Another honored cliché, but the only way you know is to go, and go, until you fail. Which is something you'll never do in ordinary life, because you never have to. Juvenile as it may sound, the only way to know your limits is to forget them.

It was five-thirty when we finished off the steeple of Waddington. The pinnacle was so sharp only one of us could stand on top at a time. For just a moment—the moment that is all and everything—the world fell away.

John and I were lucky. For a few days we traded the constant weight of responsibility for the angelic lightness of hubris. Next time? I don't know.

On the summit we opted not to bivy for fear of freezing to death and instead rapped the whole south face in the dark in a storm. We used up every piece of gear and were about to begin lopping off sections of rope to use as slings when we reached our tent. It was one in the morning.

It would take us another five days to get out, but first we spent twenty-four hours sleeping with the pinups and drinking Jim and the boys' rum. We didn't find out to whom we owed the pleasure until the flight out, when our bush pilot told us that we must have been mistaken for a Canadian military team attempting Waddington via the tried-and-true west face.

Running Stairs

He who fights with monsters should be
careful lest he thereby become a monster.
—Friedrich Nietzsche, *Beyond Good and Evil*

I have not bathed in seventy-three days.

I know this will disgust you, but this isn't anything like football
or gym class. We're sweating so hard from day one, glistening like
draft horses, that everyone smells the same. After three weeks one's
body reaches a state of equilibrium: oiled, content in its own animal
smell, heat rash where the pack straps go over the shoulders, hair mal-
leably greasy.

Since the start of the expedition, I've lost at least twenty pounds,
perhaps more. I trained hard before coming here—going to the stadium every day—so I didn't have that much to lose. Feeling my corporeal self inside my sleeping bag, beneath my foul long underwear,
I find things missing. For example, I no longer have triceps. They were
superfluous and thus consumed, leaving my shrunken biceps the only
muscle fastening elbow to shoulder. And my lattisimus dorsi, the
wings of the back, they too are gone. My pectorals, once solid plaques
of masculinity, gone too.

Of course any fat was dispatched long ago. The little slip of suet
below one's chin, the invisible pads between the legs, the pleasing
wrap around one's waist, all the physical manifestations of affluence
and boredom, dished up and devoured.

I see now that arms and chest were inconsequential. Just extra weight. All I needed were giant lungs and ceaseless legs. I grope down inside my sleeping bag and squeeze the muscles above my cold feet. Quadriceps, hamstrings, calves. Each is sculpted, hard as marble. You would be impressed.

I take a deep breath. Even up here, where we gulp at the air as if we are drowning, I can still do that. I am lucky. One of the other men has contracted pleurisy, another pulmonary edema. My lungs, on the other hand, seem to have expanded, as if somehow mutating to accommodate for the lack of oxygen. The skin across my chest is stretched taut. Every bone protrudes. I feel the curve of each rib, the small lumps and dents from injuries I acquired decades ago, perhaps the year you knew me. When I lie flat on my back I can feel the nodes of every vertebrae. My hipbones poke up into the goose down of my sleeping bag.

Ah, I hear you. Snorting phlegm up your throat, popping your knuckles like walnuts. Other people's self-indulgence offends you.

Ordinarily, I wouldn't mention any of this, but today is unusual: I have taken a rest day. Not by choice. This is my seventeenth consecutive day spent climbing between 21,000 and 25,000 feet. Everyone said I should descend to base camp and rest, that I was tempting fate, but I didn't. It now appears that that may have been a mistake. Perhaps if . . .

I'm back. I fell asleep. I'm so exhausted.

I see that my handwriting started out erect and smooth but has already degenerated. Cold does that. It's like cancer. Most people believe that it's merely low temperatures that make one cold. But at high altitude the real problem is dehydration. Melting snow is so time consuming and wearisome that you eventually start to get lazy and don't boil up as much water as you need. As you become more and more dehydrated your blood turns to syrup and can't push its essential warmth into the capillaries. That's how you lose fingers and toes.

About half this team has had something amputated from frostbite. Joe, the leader of this expedition, he lost his big toes when he was about my age. They were snipped off irregularly in some hinterland hospital leaving rough gnarls of skin that catch when he tries to pull on his wool socks. He says it has never bothered him, but I watch him, slowly picking his way down through the glacier using his ski poles for balance. He goes slow, like a dog with three legs.

I should tell you that I'm writing this letter from the north face of Mount Everest. I am the youngest member of the team. Of the original ten climbers, only four of us are still functional.

I'm lying inside a tiny red tent on a ledge at 23,000 feet. The ledge was cut from a 9,000-foot wall of ice. There is a 2,000-foot drop from this perch down to the glacier. It took us a month of climbing to get up here. Sometimes I imagine this little tent is a kite; a kite that broke loose and soared so high it disappeared above the clouds, then crashed into the side of this mountain.

I have taken a rest day because I was too weak to continue. I realize how blasphemous this admission will sound to you, but I'm not sure I can even walk.

This morning it took all I had to piss out the tent zipper. I got up on my knees, still in my sleeping bag. The slice of light that came through the tent flap stabbed my eyes and I became dizzy. Dizziness is death up here. Vertigo is death. If I had fallen forward I would have fallen off the edge, tumbling through space.

But it was all from weakness, not vertigo. I never have vertigo on a mountain. If I've been living the horizontal life for several months and look down from the top of a tall building, I will get vertigo. I think it's due to the suddenness of a mortal perspective. The horizontal life provides primarily safe, oblique panoramas. But climbing this mountain has been such slow business, you get used to living on little ledges high in the sky. You get used to looking down and having to search the glacier for a speck which you know is a tent. It's almost like being in a plane. Who gets vertigo in a plane?

After pissing I sank back into my sleeping bag and must have fallen asleep because when I opened my eyes, my cheek was frozen to the tent floor. I decided to try to read. I have already read this camp's section of *Moby-Dick*, page 263, "Of the Less Erroneous Pictures of Whales, and the True Pictures of Whaling Scenes," to page 429, "Measurement of the Whale's Skeleton." Like all the books, we ripped *Moby-Dick* into four pieces and distributed them among the different camps on the mountain—which of course means I can't read the book in order. You might think this would be annoying, but actually I have found it intriguing. Makes me see how nicely things fit together; how the present is no more than a small extension of the past; how the future is but an interesting turn on the present; everything already right there from very early on, we just don't usually see it.

I know you don't have any idea what I'm talking about. You never read books.

So. You're wondering why I'm writing you, naturally. I know you don't know a thing about mountain climbing (it's not much like football) . . .

Sorry. Fell asleep again. Something is wrong with me.

You know one feels safe inside sleep. I dreamed of green again. We're all dreaming of green, have been for weeks. We live in a world of unbearable, blinding white—so naturally we dream of green. We dream of it like we once dreamed of sex. Carnal green. Voluptuous green. Of green cottonwoods growing straight up out of the glacier. Even if we can push our bodies right to the edge, our minds are desperate for all that we have left behind.

At dinner, when we're not too tired, lying on our sides in our sleeping bags with our cold noses hidden inside steaming cups of soup, we talk about sports that make sense. Snorkeling, in deliciously warm Caribbean water. Or lawn tennis in England on the one day the clouds spread their legs. Funny no one has mentioned golf yet, all that endless soft-flowing greenness trimmed short as a woman's pubic hair. And we never talk about football. Football players don't become mountain climbers. They're two different types of people.

None of this is really what I wanted to write you about. I seem to be getting off on tangents, which, as you wouldn't know, is likely due to hypoxia.

I'll explain briefly. Hypoxia is a lack of oxygen to the brain. At this altitude you get about half the oxygen you would at sea level. Affects everybody differently. Some climbers get nauseous and vomit regularly (there's a frozen yellow glob just outside this tent). Some get searing headaches. Some get loose concentration and float a little. You have to be careful with this one. Just because your mind is floating you can sometimes start thinking your body can too and forget about gravity: but you can never forget about gravity. If mountain climbing is anything at all, it is dancing with gravity. Dark and beautiful and seductive she is. She has eyes that take your clothes off. She wants to lie down with you. She slowly slips from her dress and you see her body and she smiles and reaches up and takes your arm and her grip is suddenly heavy, so unimaginably heavy. She won't let go and you have to be willing to kick her because she's a sorcerer, a widowmaker, an executioner with tits.

You learn this quick or you don't live long climbing mountains.

Anyway, what I wanted to tell you was what happened yesterday.

It started out as just another day. I was alone, kicking the points of my crampons into the blue ice, slowly jugging the climbing ropes we had fixed on the wall. It was the sixth day in a row I'd gone up on the face carrying loads. Every day the same: up at three A.M., oatmeal, walk up the glacier in the dark under stars brilliant as fireworks—magic every time—then start up the wall. On a good day, even with a heavy load, I would reach this camp at 23,000 feet by noon and head back down.

But yesterday I felt uneasy almost from the beginning—like how you feel when you think something bad is going to happen to someone you're close to, but you don't know who, or how, and you can't do anything about it and it makes you feel raw and upset. To my surprise I started dragging about halfway up the wall. At first I tried to ignore it—which I've had more practice at since you knew me—but when it's really bad, I don't care what you used to say, it's bad. In disbelief, I was suddenly barely moving. Each step was shrinking, rising only a few inches above the last. It seemed to require extraordinary energy to move at all. I felt like I was diminishing, as if I were being absorbed by something too vast and perhaps even too kind to fight. I had to stop for every breath. I kept craning my neck around like a baby bird, looking up, searching for this little red nest on a ledge. Then I was stopping more than going. Just standing there a thousand feet in the air, straight up above the glacier, hanging on to a rope balancing on four tiny metal teeth shoved into the ice. Then I was just stopped. I don't know for how long. I was peering upward. The air was getting colder. I could feel it freezing the snot on my face. I thought I saw some sparrows flitting above me, darting, diving, swooping playfully in the dusk—but there are no sparrows at this altitude. Then it was getting dark. I couldn't believe it. Quite calmly it occurred to me that I might not make it. I couldn't see the ledge and I couldn't lift my legs and I couldn't feel my toes. It was as if I had been given an anesthetic.

I said something to myself out loud. It took a while to sink in.

"Fuck," I whispered, my mouth barely capable of forming around the word. My lips felt unattached. I started consciously breathing the word over and over very slowly, forcing myself to speak loudly.

Then something snapped and I was momentarily lucid. I thought, How dumb. I'm going to die. I'm going to freeze to death on the north face of Everest. It seemed absurd.

Then you know what I thought of? You won't believe it: running stairs. I couldn't believe it myself. Here I was, couldn't even feel my damn feet and I'm thinking of running stairs. It was a visceral thought. My body thought of it, not me. Sometime after that I managed to get my legs moving again and eventually made it to this camp.

I'm sorry, I can barely hold the pen. I have to sleep now.

Back again. My body is not working right anymore. For two months I have been fine, but apparently no longer. I wish there was someone else up on the face with me. I must try to finish this letter.

You won't remember, but it was partly because of you that I learned how to run stairs.

I was a sinewy kid. I set the junior high school sit-up record (1,589 sit-ups in half an hour). You made us do all the physical fitness tests on the bare, hardwood floor. Setting that record left me with a bleeding, six-inch abrasion along my spine, but anything was worth it for a piece of pride when we were thirteen. You knew that.

Actually, you can't take all the credit. A boy named Weichman also had a hand in the process. It was during a game of murder ball.

This was back when boys and girls did not have gym class together. There was a boys' gym and a girls' gym, both enormous three-story mausoleums with dusty yellow light coming through a thousand panes of warped glass, bleachers running all the way to the ceiling.

Murder ball was an elementary game that I don't think you thought up, although it's precisely the kind of game you would have if you could have. Perhaps theatrically named, I think now it had some very adult, real-world veracity. Take a class of thirty gangly, all-sized, ruddy-cheeked boys—some shy to the point of fainting at VD health movies, some already so abused they could take a punch from a full-grown man, the rest of us just trying to stay out of the way— randomly divide it in half, divide the gymnasium in half, put a team on either side, slowly roll five or ten hard red rubber balls down the half-court line.

The rules were simple. "Don't git hit; if you do, yer out. Don't *ever* step over the line."

The beginning was always tense. This was the part you relished. You'd clench your jaw so tight we could see the muscles in your neck. The balls would be gliding silently down that line following one after another and several brave boys from both sides would have to race to the line swerving and ducking, snatching up a ball and throwing it as hard as they could at somebody doing the same thing three feet away. Thereafter, the sides commenced to pummel each other. The fat kids or slow kids or dumb kids always went out first, often getting hit with two or three balls at once, which would send them to the floor screaming.

Although I was reasonably quick and strong, I hated this game. I think every boy hated this game except maybe the large, vicious kids who could really throw a ball and the few kids whose dads wanted them to be World Series pitchers and had taught them how to throw hard and accurate.

Anyway, one day I hit this kid Weichman in the face. I almost always threw with the fury of fear amidst a pell-mell dash, absolutely no aim, my eyes mostly closed. The ball hooked wildly to the left just when Weichman was stumbling forward, narrowly avoiding another hissing peril. He happened to be looking up. I saw his eyes right before he was hit. I could tell it hurt and for a second I wanted to yell out, "Sorry. Hey, I'm really sorry," or something foolish like that before I realized I was close to the line and about to be hurt myself. I spun on a dime and ran zigzagging away like a shell-shocked rabbit.

When the bell rang I innocently thought Weichman had forgotten all about it, although I could see his face was still red and puffy. He jumped me in the locker room. He was much bigger but I was much quicker so all in all we punched and scraped and banged each other up against the metal lockers until Weichman's face was bleeding and a crowd was gathered. Then you broke through and dragged us off to your office.

We knew what could happen. The bruises and blood were nothing now. We'd seen the perfect pattern of blisters on the rears of the tough boys who said it didn't hurt but didn't sit down even putting on their shoes.

I was frightened of you, but inside I was feeling good because Weichman, who was twice my size, hadn't killed me. This thought must have made my lips curl up.

"Why you goddamn little smartass!" you roared. You shoved Weichman out of your office bellowing, "Better quit yer fuckin cryin! And shower that blood off yer fat face," and slammed your office door and the pinup girl tacked to the inside waved.

You cornered me. "Paddlin's something pretty funny to smartfarts like you, ain't it. Well tomorrow, tomorrow'll I'll have somethin' fer you." And you slapped me in the face and opened the door and kicked me right in the anus.

I can't focus anymore. I must rest.

I just woke up. It's dark out. I am writing by headlamp. To continue.

So. I was scared all the rest of that day and through the night when things can get bad for a boy. The next day during roll call you told me to step forward.

"Saw you step yer ass cross the line yesterday, boy!" you said.

A murmur went through the kids in class. It was like a breeze that changes its shape as it moves. At first it sounded like a snicker but then it sickened and turned into a faint groan and ended in an inaudible gasp like what happens when someone is punched in the stomach. I knew what was about to happen and began to tremble and immediately forced myself to stop it.

"Go stand yer ass 'gainst that wall."

I walked rigidly across the gym floor trying to make my knees work, stopped at the wall, and turned around.

You had all the boys lined up on the half-court line. I remember your voice was kind of high-pitched, like an overexcited dog. The boys were feverish. You dumped over the box of red balls. The boys scuffled after them and of course all the balls ended up in the hands of the meanest, most accurate throwers in class. One of them gave Weichman a ball.

I decided one thing. I decided just to make sure Weichman's ball didn't hit me.

Then you blew your whistle and all the itchy kids with strong arms and frenzied faces hurled at once, but I was concentrating on Weichman. As the firestorm descended I dodged and dove and got away from a few but then I was falling and one caught me in the ear and another in the nuts and I dropped fast and felt hot and vomit started to come up in my throat. For a moment I thought I saw sparrows above me, darting and diving, but I couldn't figure out how they got inside the gymnasium. Then your black leather shoes shoved up under my face.

"Well. Git up."

I looked up.

"Don't you give me that fuckin' grin!" And I saw your leather feet twitch as if you were going to kick me in the face. The entire gymnasium went quiet.

"You got stairs for one whole fuckin' month. Startin' now."

You dragged me to my feet by my ears and shoved me off. That's when I knew you liked me. And all the kids knew I got the gift of stairs because I'd managed not to get killed by Weichman and not to get the paddle either by not crying.

I have to tell you that you were one of the worst people I've ever met in my life. You were cruel and perverted. Despicable. But, I did learn how to run stairs from you. And I've been running them ever since.

Three months before every expedition I start visiting the university stadium. It is a mile away and I run there every day. It is a ritual. I stand in the middle of the empty football field. I stare up at the crude, invisible crowd. I hear them whistling and hooting. Then I take off. I run stairs until I can't. Until I can't lift my legs.

I have to sleep now.

Tombstone White

We left the moraine and crossed onto the glacier. It was speckled with black stones that had plummeted down the Matterhorn's east face. Some were small as fists, some big as barrels, but all had fallen thousands of feet at a fatal velocity. The glacier was gravity's missile range and we moved across it as quickly as we could. Halfway through we spotted something strange on the ice. We didn't know what it was at first—or didn't want to know. From a distance it was a contorted blue lump with blond hair. We approached holding our breath.

It was just a backpack. The impact of the fall had burst the nylon sack like a water balloon, strewing its contents across the glacier. A dented 35mm camera with a smashed lens. A down coat tied in a bundle with string. Wool socks. A woman's wool sweater melted into the ice. The pack had crash-landed here days, maybe weeks, earlier. The blond locks were loops of rope slumped out of the rucksack.

John knelt beside the shredded pack. I knew what he was thinking: *And the person who was wearing the pack?*

"Perhaps she took it off to rest," I said, "and the pack just slipped over the edge."

We continued up the Furgg glacier to the icefall, deciding to climb directly up the middle rather than hike the big loop around the end. Foreshortening is the mother of all optimism, and shortcuts seldom are, but certain kinds of people—mountaineers in particular—have a tendency to choose the hope of the unknown over the reality of the well trodden. We soon became lost in a labyrinth of wide-mouthed crevasses and leaning seracs, and had to rope up and slow down. We began to zigzag radically, searching for the firmest-looking snowbridges.

A helicopter suddenly appeared overhead and made passes back and forth above the icefall. We were afraid the pilot thought we were in need of a rescue. Then the helicopter arced backward and landed on the mountain far below us. Minutes later it flew over us again, this time with an orange-suited human harnessed to a cable swinging beneath the aircraft. The chopper gradually lowered the person onto the Matterhorn's east face, right at the top of the icefall. We got out the monocular. The helicopter backed away from the wall, the cable dangling like an empty fishing line. For the next few minutes it circled, then dropped back in against the east face and hovered briefly. When it flew back into the blue sky, there was another human harnessed to the end of the line, a limp body with limbs hanging in unnatural positions.

The year before I had come to Zermatt to climb the north face of the Matterhorn and it had snowed ceaselessly for six days. Still, I thought I could cajole a local climber into making a quick trip up the Hornli Ridge, the mountain's autobahn, the route climbed by unskilled hordes every summer. But not one climber was interested. I tracked down several guides, all of whom shook their heads. "No one. No one guides Matterhorn when it snows," said one veteran bergführer who had climbed the mountain over 200 times.

I hiked up beyond the Hornli hut alone and found over a foot of snow on the route and the rocks so slippery it was as if the mountain had been coated in grease. I descended, chastened.

Now, a year later, I was back with a partner, John Harlin, with whom I had climbed Mount Waddington. The north face was loaded with unconsolidated, avalanche-prone snow, and John had climbed the Hornli Ridge on a previous trip, so we decided to attempt a traverse: trek halfway around the mountain, crossing from Switzerland into Italy, ascend the Italian Ridge, cross over the 14,690-foot summit, and descend via the Hornli. The hike over to the south side of the

massif would give us a chance to acclimatize and the weather a
chance to shape up.

After the helicopter disappeared with the body (we later learned it
was that of a Polish climber who had fallen off the Hornli Ridge),
John and I finished the icefall, topping out on the Furggen Ridge. We
spent the night there, at 10,957 feet, in the Bossi *refugio*, a tiny, filthy,
round-topped aluminum hut that is depressingly similar to a sheep-
herder's trailer. We boiled soup and spoke softly, reassuring each other
that the man we'd seen had died because he had made a mistake, a
mistake we wouldn't have made—this is the bedtime lie that consoles
all climbers.

In the morning it was much colder, the barometer sinking, the
mountain lost in mist. We dropped down onto the stone-speckled
Cervino Glacier, crossed below the south face, and started up the Italian Ridge just as it began to snow. The air filled with snowflakes as big
as leaves, the wind roared in, and before long we found ourselves in
a full-on blizzard. What was supposed to be a simple scramble up to
the Carrel hut at 12,562 feet on the Italian Ridge turned into a half-
desperate dance over slick rocks skidding out from under our feet.
The thick chain hanging down the famous Whymper Chimney,
placed there to aid in the ascent of the rock corner, was encased in ice.
When we got to the hut our eyelids were frozen open and our jaws
frozen shut.

There was an experienced Czech team inside. They showed us a
personalized journal that documented all the ascents they'd done
across Europe. You could feel the vertigo in the photos. They had been
waiting out the weather for several days; periodically one of them
would step outside, then come back in covered with snow and
cussing flamboyantly, making his teammates laugh.

The blizzard continued through the afternoon and into the

evening, as one team after another arrived at the Carrel hut. The door would burst open and a blast of snow would blow in a frost-covered climber, crampons on his feet, an ice axe in each hand, beard crusted white. Stabbing his crampons into the wooden floor, he would flip a glazed rope over his shoulder, brace himself, and begin reeling his partners—one by one, each an abominable snowman—into the hut. By nightfall there were twenty climbers crowding the shelter and the walls were covered with dripping jackets and wet wool sweaters. Outside, the storm intensified, furious that we had found someplace to hide.

In the morning the storm was gone, the sun was up and the Matterhorn was buried in snow. We all slept in, assuming the mountain would be unassailable. One more check mark on the "failed" side of the ledger. It's a part of mountaineering you have to get used to, even though you never do because if you did you'd quit climbing.

A French guide proclaimed the Matterhorn unclimbable. He was taking his two clients down immediately. I asked him what he thought about the chances of the mountain coming back into condition in a few days, and he replied that in a few days the sun would turn the snow to ice and the mountain would become coated in sheets of verglas and thus *traître extrêmement!*—extremely treacherous. Furthermore, the weather forecast called for another storm in the next two days.

A snow-plastered mountain, a French guide's knowing opinion, and a bad forecast. That was it. That was enough.

The French guide and his clients went down. The Czech team went down. Two Spanish teams and two other Czech teams that had arrived the evening before went down. Everybody went down but John and me and a father and son team that had arrived so late the night before they were spending the day in their sleeping bags.

John and I stood on the airy steel veranda and watched the retreat. Going down wasn't easy. The Carrel hut is perched high on a thin arête, the emptiness of the west face dropping off to one side, the blankness of the south face to the other. The climbers rappelled right off the hut stanchions, sliding into space.

Jean-Antoine Carrel is the climber who was forgotten when Edward Whymper successfully climbed the Matterhorn on July 14, 1865. Carrel, born in 1829 in Breuil, the Italian hamlet below the south face of the Matterhorn, was one of the Alps's founding mountain guides and the first man possessed with the vision and the will to try to scale the Matterhorn. His first attempt was in 1857; he tried again in 1858 and 1861. He made three more attempts in 1862, two of them with Whymper. Whymper and Carrel were friends and rivals. Carrel the tough, grizzled chamois hunter; versus Whymper, the twenty-five-year-old English artist, a climbing rookie burning with the desire to summit the stone dagger that had been pronounced unclimbable.

There were seventeen attempts made on the Matterhorn, eight of them by Whymper himself, before the Englishman pulled it off. It was a battle of egos and shifting loyalties. Carrel considered the Matterhorn his mountain, jealously coveted the summit, and viewed Whymper as an interloper. Whymper believed Carrel to be the best climber in the Alps and had actually arranged to hire him for what turned out to be his successful ascent. But during the week of Whymper's planned attempt, bad weather intervened, and Carrel secretly agreed to guide a four-man, all-Italian team, leaving Whymper out in the cold. When the Englishman discovered that Carrel was attempting the mountain from the Italian side, he hurriedly cobbled together a seven-man team in Zermatt to make an attempt from the Swiss side.

On the summit day, Whymper's party ascended the Hornli

Ridge, while the Carrel team climbed the Italian Ridge on the opposite side of the mountain. Carrel had gotten a late start, and the Italian Ridge is the more difficult route, but Whymper won the race by
only 600 feet. When he stood on the summit, Whymper could see
Carrel and his companions below him. He trundled off a few stones
to get their attention. Carrel looked up and was crestfallen. He
turned back, only to return three days later, with a new team, to successfully complete the first ascent of the Italian Ridge and the second
ascent of the Matterhorn.

Whymper's victory, however, exacted a grievous cost. During the
descent, four members of his group fell to their deaths. One man,
Douglas Hadow, slipped, pulling off three others. Whymper and his
two guides, Peter Taugwalder Sr. and Peter Taugwalder Jr., caught the
fall, but the rope snapped and Michel Croz, a Chamonix guide, and
the English climbers Charles Hudson, Douglas Hadow, and Francis
Douglas fell 4,000 feet.

In Zermatt, Taugwalder Sr. and Whymper were accused of cutting
the rope. The Swiss authorities conducted an inquest. After three days,
Whymper and Taugwalder were exonerated, but the controversy continued. The *Times* of London denounced the ascent and deplored the
utter uselessness of the sport of mountaineering. Queen Victoria considered outlawing the climbing of mountains. European newspapers
published denunciatory editorials by writers who had never set foot
on any mountain, let alone the Matterhorn. England was in an uproar
over the disaster and everyone had an opinion. (Sound familiar?)

In 1871, Whymper gave his account of the story in a best-selling
book titled *Scrambles Amongst the Alps*. Whymper would be famous for the
rest of his life, although he hardly climbed in the Alps again. He went
to Greenland, then to the Andes with Carrel, then to the Canadian
Rockies.

Deaths of a putatively heroic nature seem to have a bizarre magnetism, particularly for those who have never witnessed the horror of

dying. In Whymper's wake, everybody wanted to climb the Matterhorn. (Sound familiar?) In 1871 an English adventuress named Lucy Walker became the first woman to summit the mountain. The Zmutt Ridge was climbed by the famous English alpinist Albert Frederick Mummery in 1879. In 1881, twenty-three-year-old Teddy Roosevelt climbed the mountain. In 1911, the Matterhorn's last remaining unconquered ridge, the Furggen, was ascended. The north and south faces fell in 1931.

Thousands have attempted the Matterhorn, and more than 450 have died—more than on Everest or McKinley, Rainier or the Grand Teton. Technically, both the Italian Ridge and the Hornli Ridge are far more difficult than the trade routes up these other peaks. Whymper's and Carrel's achievements are a testament to the skill and determination of mountaineering's earliest pioneers.

After turning tail on the Matterhorn the first time, I took a walk through the Zermatt cemetery, the graveyard of the Matterhorn. There are tombstones with ice axes and ropes sculpted into the rock, tombstones with actual axes and crampons bolted onto the stone, even a tombstone in which a crucified Christ is adorned as a climber, axe and rope hanging from his body. These are the graves of too many who attempted the Matterhorn and paid for it with their lives. But the arrogant and the unprepared lie side by side with great guides who also died on the mountain—Alois Graven, Johann Biner, Isidor Perren, Hermann Perren. The Matterhorn is indiscriminate. (Jean-Antoine Carrel, who perished in a blizzard on the Matterhorn in 1890, is notably absent; his final resting place is Valtournanche, in the shadow of the mountain's Italian side.)

Whymper ends *Scrambles Amongst the Alps* with this admonition: "Climb if you will, but remember that courage and strength are nought without prudence, and that a momentary negligence may destroy the happiness of a lifetime. Do nothing in haste; look well to each step; and from the beginning think what may be the end."

Walking past those tombstones at dusk, with their hats of fresh powder, I understood why they don't guide when it snows on the Matterhorn.

John and I shoveled the snow off the bench outside the Carrel hut and took turns staring up at the Italian Ridge with a monocular. It didn't look that bad. It really didn't. There was a lot of new snow, but it was melting fast.

Sometimes it doesn't pay to think too much; other times thinking will save your life. It's case by case. The hard part is knowing what is reality and what is just the confusion of opinion, hearsay, and the constant three-way battle in your head between Mr. Ego, Mr. Fear, and Mr. Rational. If you can't sort it out, you can get killed. Of course, you can get killed even if you do sort it out.

By noon we couldn't stand it anymore.

"We could just run up a few pitches and see how it goes," John blurted.

"Right," I chimed. "If it's bad, we can rap right back down."

To forestall an imprudent attempt on the summit, neither of us took food or water. John even left his headlamp behind. We were going for a little reconnaissance, nothing more.

With all the snow and us not knowing the route, we moved cautiously, but steadily, and in three hours found ourselves atop Tyndal Point with only the last rock tower between us and the summit. We were standing right where Carrel had stood—only a few hours from the top—when Whymper had summited. We cursed our own late start. We cursed the unwarranted foreboding we had allowed into our hearts. We cursed our prudence for tricking ourselves into leaving behind food and water.

What's done is done. We descended to the Carrel hut.

The next morning we were up at four, cruising the lower portions of the Italian Ridge at six, attacking the icy summit block at eight, snapping pictures on the hanging ladder at ten, standing on the summit at noon.

Then, with perfect timing, the storm hit.

It was colder than the storm two days before. Winds that could knock us off our feet, bullets of snow, zero visibility. The mountain was instantly sheeted with ice, making it impossible to downclimb. We started to rappel, one anchor down to the next. The first rap off the summit we ran into a three-man Italian team who had also summited. The day before, one of their teammates had turned around, taking their second rope with him. Their one rope, doubled, didn't reach between the rappel anchors, so they were each rapping off the end of the rope and then soloing down to the next anchor—absurdly dangerous behavior, given the conditions.

Sometimes your own random good fortune can be another man's salvation. Someone had left a climbing rope in the Carrel hut and John and I had taken it with us, just in case we needed an extra. The Italians would have hugged us if we hadn't all been clinging to the side of the mountain.

It took John and me almost five hours to make it down to the Solvay emergency hut at 13,133 feet on the Hornli Ridge. We were soaking wet and shivering. It wasn't a true emergency, but we didn't want it to become one.

"Well, John," I said, plucking the icicles from my eyebrows, "should we stay or should we go?"

"Tomorrow it could be storming even harder."

"Tomorrow the sun could come out."

"Mark, we can make it down tonight."

"If we get off route it'll be a cold bivy."

In the end, we decided to humbly stay the night, our fourth on a mountain that is supposed to be climbed in one day. The Italians came stumbling in an hour later.

In the morning it was clear and sunny. We descended to the Hornli hut, a comfortingly huge hostel-cum-restaurant. The Italians bought us beers and we all sat in awe of the gleaming gothic cathedral of the Alps.

Other teams had been going up the mountain as we were coming down. A speedy Austrian team. A somber, silent German team. An American talking to his wife on a cell phone, maintaining he was doing just fine. (She was saying he was way behind schedule for the little distance he'd ascended, and should turn around. She was right.) And a Japanese team. The Japanese were all bunched together except for one guy in silly nylon boots and ill-fitting clothes, climbing clumsily and unroped, apparently trying to stay ahead of his teammates.

Several hours later he died falling off the Matterhorn.

Ego Trip

At the eleventh hour, the day before departure, my partner bailed. Something hadn't been right from the beginning—the tone of his voice on the phone, the odd nonchalance toward planning our gear and food. I felt it in my gut but ignored the signals. We almost always know what's really going on, we just don't want to admit it.

I hardly remember the excuse now. A job interview? Or was it his girlfriend, his mother, money—it doesn't matter. An excuse is just that. At the last minute, he wasn't going. The question was, was I?

The plane ticket was in my pocket, pack packed, time carved off the calendar. I could have canceled, but I was itching for another expedition. Besides, I'd told my friends I was off to Bolivia to climb. I boarded the plane early the next morning and ordered two beers to toast my resolve.

In the prideful world of international climbing, South America isn't cool. The Himalayas are cool. They've got cachet. They're celebrity mountains, shiny and famous as Brad Pitt. Say you're off to Nepal or Tibet and you're immediately conferred a certain exaltedness. People who know nothing about you suddenly become envious. But want to know a secret? South America is better. No permits, no peak fees, no porters. No feckless bureaucrats, no avaricious liaison officers, and best of all, no endless weeks of headachy acclimatization just to slog another mile higher in the sky. South America is cheaper, more accessible, and more fun. What's more, your chances of summiting are higher. You just have to decide whether you're climbing for the sake of climbing, or to impress people.

Bolivia is a hard brown landscape beneath a harsh blue sky, just like Wyoming. I felt right at home. I got a high-ceilinged pension in the old quarter of La Paz. Every morning I did my pull-ups on a pipe in the bathroom, then laced on my boots and ran from the mercado, at 12,000 feet, up to the 14,000-foot rim of the altiplano. Past the peeling European buildings with their tiny balconies and tall shutters, up through the trim, whitewashed homes of the middle class and into the vast shantytown of tin, plywood, and plastic. Atop the altiplano I'd stop to stare eastward at the Cordillera Real, a white spine of 6,000-meter peaks, then descend back into the haze of the city, moving fast, working the thighs. Back at the mercado I'd put away a half-dozen Quechuan tacos, three bottles of Fanta, and a banana.

In the afternoons I traipsed from one pension to another hunting for a new climbing partner. I was certain I'd find one. Expeditions are always falling apart—illness, injury, or attitude will knock out two or three people and pretty soon the whole trip is in shambles. I figured I'd have my pick of alpinists. But it wasn't so. The few Americans I found were either aimless, dreadlocked pilgrims or eager but inexperienced clients of guided climbs. All the Euro teams seemed to have it together. A four-man Austrian expedition was heading for 20,873-foot Illampu, their packs so small it looked as if they were on a day hike. Two experienced Spaniards, inseparable partners, were bound for Ancohuma. A Swiss-French team shut the door when I peeked into their room. There was a Japanese expedition that filled up two floors of a pension—one floor for all the climbers, the other for their gear. They wanted me to join their team. I declined. Ditto an offer from three Koreans who had spanking new gear but didn't know how to start their stove. Both teams struck me as overly zealous, so focused on the summit they might be tempted to take unjustifiable risks.

Down a cobblestone alley in a shabby hotel I found a three-woman, two-man Slovenian team going to 18,531-foot Condoriri to attempt a new route. They were confident and relaxed. They pulled me into their cramped room to drink wine with them while they loaded piles of Russian ice screws into their worn packs. Their leader was a tall, svelte woman named Ada. She wore a tank top and purple tights. You could see the muscles in her thighs as she moved around. She had flaming auburn hair, prominent cheekbones, and eyes so ravishing I was too self-conscious to look straight at her.

"So, where is partner?" Ada asked me.

"I came to Bolivia alone."

"Ahhh, I see." She pushed her hair back and lowered her Cleopatra eyes on me. "You come to solo. Very good."

The other four members of her team nodded at me in respect and admiration. One climber, a towering guy with stringy hair and a nose that had obviously been broken, gave me the thumbs-up.

"Stefan also solos," said Ada, smirking at her teammate.

I'd never intended to solo anything on this trip. I intended to find a partner, preferably one stronger and more experienced than myself. Although I had soloed mountains in the past, soloing was something that took a stronger head than I had. Soloing required gravitas. No backup, no net—one mistake and you die. I didn't have the screwed-up childhood or soul-wrenching angst or any other usefully twisted motivation for soloing. I also didn't have the cojones. But now I had this instant reputation.

"And what are you going to climb?" Ada continued.

My erstwhile partner and I had talked about a dozen different mountains but hadn't settled on anything. On my morning runs I'd studied the two peaks just outside La Paz, 21,201-foot Illimani and 20,340-foot Huanya Potosí. The trade routes on both were known to be interesting and not too technical.

"Huayna Potosí," I declared.

Ada arched her razor eyebrows and a shadow of disappointment crossed her face.

"The east face," I heard myself say, and they all broke into toothy grins and shook their heads in approval and my tin cup was refilled with red wine.

"To your climb," said Ada, winking and batting her eyelashes.

I sometimes think back and wonder if she actually knew, somehow, that I'd made it all up on the spot. Nah, of course not. She was just winking at me because she knew she was beautiful and because beautiful women always like bold mountaineers, particularly beautiful women who *are* bold mountaineers.

That night I went to a good restaurant, La Carreta, ordered myself a big Argentine steak, and drank one cold beer after another until I was convinced that climbing the east face of Huayna Potosí was indeed exactly what I'd come to do. Although, having no guidebook and no topo, I had no idea if such a route even existed.

I slipped out of my pension before dawn, my pack banging the French doors on the way out, my intentions murky. I walked Avenida Ismael Montes up out of La Paz. From the altiplano, most of Huayna Potosí was buried in clouds, but the summit was still visible. I decided to hitchhike my way toward it. Ten minutes later I hopped into the bed of a giant truck to discover five dust-covered Quechua farmers clad in pointed caps and bright serapes.

By noon we had rumbled into the clouds. Big wet flakes swirled like miniature paratroopers into the bed of the truck. The driver stopped in a muddy mining town. He wanted money. Being the obvious rich guy, I gave him a few bills. The road ended only a few miles further on, at a stone dam holding back a reservoir of black water. The farmers slung their baskets onto their backs and walked off. I couldn't believe there was tillable soil anywhere—all I could see through the snow were walls of wet rock. I tiptoed along the half-moon rim of the dam. The falling snow seemed bright and carefree until it hit the reservoir and vanished into the foreboding blackness. I followed an aqueduct for some distance, then a snowy trail up to a frozen tarn.

There were two tents in the talus beside the pond. I got my tent up and had just crawled inside when there came a tap-tapping at my nylon door. I unzipped the flap and in came a steaming mug of coffee.

"Welcome, American," said a voice with a Slavic accent.

I stuck my head out. It was almost dark. All I could make out was the figure of a broad-shouldered man. I took a drink of the coffee. It was heavily spiked—half coffee, half vodka.

"Russian?" I asked.

"Ach, you offend me."

"Sorry." I knew better than to make a wild guess.

"Czech."

His name was Petar and within five minutes I was jammed into his tent along with three of his companions. Two climbers in their team had not yet arrived. In the past few days they had reconned the entire lower portion of the east face. I listened intently, taking mental notes of their descriptions of the seracs, crevasses, and hanging glaciers.

"But now with this storm," said Petar, shrugging, "the crevasses will be hidden."

It snowed again the next day. We hung out in our tents swapping tales of previous climbs. That night the weather cleared. On the third day we all stayed in camp, giving the snow a chance to settle. I was preparing to ask if I could join their gallant team, when the two remaining climbers showed up. Hugs all around and mugfuls of killer coffee. I was introduced.

"Americaner! Slovenes told us. You come to solo east face."

I hadn't leaked a word to my new Czech friends about this ill-begotten rumor. I'd assumed it had disappeared when I did.

Petar slapped me on the back, grinning. "So, Mark, you have been holding your program from us!"

"No, no . . ." I laughed. I faltered.

All I had to do was tell the truth. I might lose face, but at least this house of cards would be toppled. I took a big slug of coffee. I was about to explain when Petar made an impromptu toast.

"To your climb!"

They crashed mugs and shouted.

That night the sky was thick with stars. I lay in my tent staring up through the half-opened flap. It was going to be a perfect morning. I was acclimatized. I was as strong as I'd ever been in my life. In a few hours I would have to confess, or climb.

I woke before my alarm went off and dressed by headlamp, still inside my dream. Two men were ascending the side of a mountain in a snowstorm. They were identical twins, but one was young, the other old. They were arguing.

"If it gets too bad, we can just turn around," yelled the young one.

The older climber, his face darkly sunburned, shook his head and stopped. "You can't always just turn around."

The young climber kept moving up, tugging on the rope.

"It's not safe," shouted the old man.

"Safe? It's never safe," said the young climber dismissively.

I listened, packing my rucksack by rote. Down coat, spare mittens, water bottle, sardines, cashews, jackknife.

I downed a liter of water and a bar of chocolate. As if someone had turned down the volume, their debate began to fade. It was academic. The decision had already been made.

I sorted through my gear. Rope or no rope. Pro or no pro. Rope and protection go together; it's either all or nothing. I made a pile—harness, biners, screws, slings, nuts, cams, rope—and lifted it up. Too heavy. Forget it.

I crawled out of the tent, fastened two ice tools and my crampons to the pack, and started up the talus in the moonlight. I'd gone 300 yards when I stopped, turned around, and walked back to camp. Sometimes second thoughts are not a sign of timidity, but of sagacity. Sometimes second thoughts save your life.

I cut the pile in half. It's never all or nothing. A handful of slings, three ice screws, three nuts, and a 200-foot length of 5mm Kevlar.

Even with the new snow, I could see a faint trail zigzagging up the ridge. I moved fast, bounding from one boulder to the next. There were glaciers on either side of the ridge, twisted and sharp, like rivers of broken glass. I stayed on the arête, reaching the top by daybreak. The mountain was before me, bathed in pink. The warm light made the walls of snow and ice appear inviting, benign. I popped on my crampons and set off up the glacier.

The sheering angle of the sun was perfect. I could detect the slightest dip in the snow. To the right and left were open crevasses. I traced each avulsion until it squeezed shut, then followed the faint trough to where it intersected my line of ascent. Climbing with one tool in each hand, I made tigerlike leaps every time I thought I was at the edge of a concealed hole. The snow was so stiff and clean, my crampons barely left tracks. Everything seemed to be going smoothly. Whenever I looked up I could see my route: across the glacier, S-curves around two icefalls, straight up the headwall, onto the unseen summit.

I was moving around the second icefall when I had the eerie feeling I was being watched, instinctively looked over my shoulder, and gasped. Clouds. Not just clouds but a black cloud bank. The front must have crept up from the Amazon, stealthy and quiet as an assassin. I had been so focused on getting to the summit I hadn't even noticed.

I quickened my pace, jumping crevasses almost recklessly. The front unnerved me. In twenty minutes its ominous shadow began to obscure the light I needed to detect the hidden crevasses. The atmosphere of the climb suddenly changed. Roped to a partner it would have been no big deal. Solo, I started to get scared. But I was less than 2,000 feet from the summit—maybe two hours away.

When I got to the steep headwall there was a gaping bergshrund and it was snowing. This was the time and place to turn around. If I turned back right here, right now, I could still find my tracks down the face and be back in camp for breakfast with the Czechs. Two big cups of Slavic coffee, sans the coffee, tell the whole bloody truth at lunch. But I was on autopilot. My ego had taken over the controls.

I walked along the jaw of ice to where it attached to the wall, chose my spot, and leapt, slamming picks and front points into the wall. The ice was ideal—soft as wood. I skittered up the face like a frightened spider, calves and forearms aching. When I gained the ridge the summit was still almost visible. I could even discern the swooping lines of buried crevasses. I was climbing as fast as I could. At a lower elevation I would have been running. I swung only one tool and made my legs do the work. I moved like a machine. I thought only about the summit. Twice I stood on the lower lip of a steep crevasse, leaned out, sunk both tools in the upper lip, and cranked over the blue-mouthed abyss.

I am ashamed to report that I successfully summited Huayna Potosí. On top it was snowing so hard I couldn't see fifty feet. And yet I had a perfect view of my own conceit: it was inexcusable to have kept going and now getting down was going to be mortally dangerous.

Off the summit pyramid I jumped the crevasses with a combination of dread and determination. I used up all the slings setting V-thread rappels to escape down the headwall. I used up all the ice screws and nuts doing desperate self-belays across the minefield of crevasses. Every rappel, every belay, was made off just one anchor. The entire descent, even more than the ascent, was unjustifiably risky.

When I finally stepped off the glacier onto the rock ridge—safe—the tension in my chest collapsed, my legs gave out from under me, and I crumpled into the talus.

Surviving by the skin of your teeth is the stuff of legend. These are the war stories we boast of to our buddies, as if survival alone were vindication. But it is not. Just because I summited and managed to get down alive doesn't mean I did the right thing. I'd been a fool. I'd made bad decisions for the wrong reasons since the day I stepped onto the plane. Surviving after a series of stupid moves means nothing more than that the gods took pity on you. It's nothing to brag about.

When I could walk again I started picking my way down the ridge, stopping a lot, staying on the trail. I was talking out loud to myself. I swore, over and over, I'd never do something like this again. "Are you listening, Mark?" I'd yell, and then I'd clap myself on the side of the head.

I promised myself that when I got back to camp I wouldn't say a word to the Czechs. If they asked I'd say I'd gone out for a hike, a little recon. I'd tell them I'd changed my mind about a solo climb, that it was too dangerous, that I was going home. I wouldn't turn what I'd done into some kind of guy-on-the-summit-arms-in-the-air hero story. I wouldn't.

Petar was standing outside his tent when I trudged into camp.

"Marco! You did it, didn't you!"

I held my tongue but I was already grinning. I wouldn't. I swore I wouldn't.

Breathless Heights

I am suffocating. The thought transfuses into me intravenously. It is cave-black and hot and wet and my arms are bound along my sides. I don't understand what's happening. I jerk my head around to find a hooded assailant behind me. He has pulled a plastic bag over my head and twisted it around my neck. I am struggling violently, trying to scream, my neck bulging, my mouth stretched wide open but there's no air. I begin to go weak. I can't believe this is how I will die, so quickly, my brain exploding and my lungs collapsing, all for a simple lack of oxygen . . .

I wake. My head is thrown back, my chest heaving. The sweat-drenched sleeping bag is twisted like a tourniquet around my torso. I release one arm and grope for my headlamp. I check the time, find my notepad and pencil: "Night 13, 23:35, 13.6% O2, 18,200 ft, can't breathe, hellish headache."

I take a swallow from my water bottle, force myself to take another, kick off the sleeping bag, and try to fall back to sleep. The thumping in my skull is so piercing that the blood itself seems to ache. I attempt to relax. Concentrate on breathing. In . . . out. In . . . out. But the moment I begin to doze off, the primordial binary rhythm of breathing that is automatic and unconscious at lower elevations becomes shallow and irregular. Once again I start to smother, then, like a dolphin surging up out of the ocean, I burst from murky half-dreams desperately trying to catch my breath.

I know what's happening. I've been through this before, on Aconcagua, Everest, Xixabangma, even Kilimanjaro. I have AMS, acute mountain sickness. I ascended too quickly—the cardinal mountaineering mistake—and now I'm paying. Severe headache, shortness of breath, sleep apnea (unconscious cessation of breathing), with fatigue, dizziness, and violent bouts of nausea still left to look forward to. All of these symptoms may pass, or they may not; AMS is a fickle torturer. There's only one sure cure: descent. It's the middle of the night and I am loath to lose altitude, but my body is clearly telling me that I'm not yet capable of sleeping at 18,200 feet. No sleep tonight and tomorrow I'll feel hollow-headed, agitated, buzzy—the perfect mental malaise for screwing up.

I reluctantly swing my feet out of my sleeping bag, open the door, and step out of the oxygen-deprivation chamber.

Climb high, sleep low. That has been the mountaineer's maxim for a century. The old paradigm: get to the base of your chosen massif, set up base camp, start ferrying loads. Up for the day, down for the night. Put in Camps I, II, III, or more over the course of several weeks, giving your physiology plenty of time to acclimatize. Then, when the clouds clear, blast for the summit. With skill, tenacity, stamina, and strength (in that order), you may come home. Throw in good luck and good weather and you may come home having summited. Throw in a good partner and a sense of humor and you may come home having actually enjoyed yourself.

A thousand feet a day—another mountain climbing canon. Thus mountains in the 15,000-to-19,000-foot range would take about a week; 20,000-to-25,000-foot peaks, three weeks; 8,000-meter peaks (the fourteen mountains that rise above 26,250 feet), six weeks or more—not because of the technical difficulty of the climbing or the number of feet to be ascended, but simply because the average human body requires that much time to adjust to the lack of oxygen at high altitude.

Enter the new paradigm: speed. If the Eiger could be done in eight days, why not seven, or three, or one. The record for climbing the north face of the Eiger is now less than seven hours. That's fine for summits under 16,000 feet. But on the high peaks, genetics have gotten in the way of modern man's ever-accelerating pursuit of acceleration. Humans evolved at or near sea level, where the air is 78 percent nitrogen, 21 percent oxygen, and 1 percent trace gases such as argon and carbon dioxide. Along with food and water, oxygen is necessary to keep our body's 100 trillion cells alive. Like a sophisticated, finely tuned engine, the human body is calibrated to perform optimally at 21 percent oxygen at 14.7 pounds of atmospheric pressure per square inch—that is, at sea level. Drive the average human machine up 10,000 or 20,000 feet and it will start sputtering and choking like a car with a maladjusted carburetor. Although the relative percentage of oxygen in the air remains constant, the higher you go, the more the air pressure drops—and the more the pressure of oxygen drops in turn. Imagine a column of air five or six miles high. At the bottom of the column—sea level—the weight of all the air above compresses the air below. This dense air is rich in oxygen. Halfway up the column, at around 18,000 feet, there's half the pressure, and thus half the oxygen. Near the top of the column—say, on the summit of Everest (29,028 feet)—there's only one third the pressure that exists at sea level and thus only one third the oxygen.

For years mountain climbers have been attempting to pre-acclimatize—hiking, climbing, skiing, or just hanging out at elevations lower than their goal but higher than their home. Doing a few fourteeners before heading for Mount Foraker, scrambling in the Alps before climbing in the Andes. Still, although these pre-climb climbing trips have sharpened many an alpinist's mountain acumen and technical skill, they are usually too short in duration to effectively jump-start physiological acclimatization. The only way to acclimatize for high-altitude mountaineering has been the slow way: go up high and stay there until you stop puking.

Until now.

"Contrary to popular belief, it was proven back in the 1970s that living and training at moderate or high altitude did not produce faster endurance athletes," says cardiologist Ben Levine, director of the Institute for Exercise and Environmental Medicine in Dallas, who spent a year living in Nepal working for the Himalayan Rescue Association. "Any beneficial acclimatization effect was detrimentally offset by the inability to train at high intensity due to the lack of oxygen."

Humans can survive without food for three weeks, without water for three days, but without oxygen for barely three minutes. When you first go to high altitude (defined by Levine as 3,000 meters— almost 10,000 feet—or above), the dearth of oxygen catapults the body into a state of emergency. Respiration and heart rate escalate immediately, straining to deliver oxygen. The kidneys, sensitive monitors of our blood chemistry, react by secreting a hormone called erythropoietin (EPO), which stimulates the production of extra red blood cells in the bone marrow. These are the tractor-trailers that haul the fuel (oxygen) from the source (lungs) to the power plants (cell mitochondria). Put more tractor-trailers on the highway and you'll be able to burn more fuel, substantially boosting endurance and power. (More red blood cells is exactly what blood doping and synthetic EPO injections create, hence the suppurating controversy in some sports, particularly road cycling.) Although going from sea level to the top of a fourteener will temporarily stimulate the kidneys to increase EPO threefold, the importance of this increase to mountain climbing pales in comparison to increasing your blood oxygen level simply by breathing harder and faster—otherwise known as ventilatory acclimatization.

"Fifteen years ago, after studying the current literature, it occurred to us that there might be a way to get the best of both worlds," says Levine. "That is, have athletes live at moderate altitude, taking advantage of the improved oxygen transport system, but train at low altitude, where the extra oxygen would allow for maximal workouts."

With colleague James Stray-Gundersen, and funded by the U.S. Olympic Committee, Levine set out in 1989 to test his hypothesis. For seven years the team conducted multiple experiments with elite American endurance athletes—some living and training at moderate altitude (Deer Valley, Utah, 7,200 feet), some living and training at sea level (San Diego), and some living at moderate altitude (Deer Valley) but training at a lower altitude (Salt Lake City, 4,390 feet). In 1997 Levine and Stray-Gundersen published their findings in the *Journal of Applied Physiology* in an influential paper titled "Living High—Training Low."

"What we found then," says Levine, "and have confirmed in subsequent studies, is that athletes who live at moderate altitude but train at low altitude can improve performance at sea level by 1 to 3 percent." In other words, living high and training low turns out to be a legal, natural, noninvasive form of blood doping. (Whether it is ethical or not is another question.)

At about the same time, Heikki Rusko, a sports scientist from Finland, reported similar results, although his method of bringing endurance athletes up and down in altitude was dramatically different. Finland is as flat as the lakes that cover it, so Rusko built "nitrogen huts" to simulate high altitude. These huts reduced the availability of oxygen not by altering the atmospheric pressure, but by simply pumping in more nitrogen to alter the oxygen-nitrogen ratio. Again, athletes increased their performance by 1 to 3 percent.

Which may not seem like much until you realize that in the 10,000 meters (10K) at the 2000 Olympics, the difference between the Gold Medal, won by Ethiopian Haile Gebrselassie in 27:18:20, and tenth place, taken by American Abdihakim Abdirahman in 27:46.17, was less than 3 percent. The difference between Lance Armstrong's winning time in the 2001 Tour de France (86:17:28) and the time of the 100th place finisher, Florent Brard (88:54:33), was also less than 3 percent.

"Put it this way," says Larry Kutt, owner of Colorado Altitude Training (CAT). "In the world of professional endurance athletics, 3 percent is the difference between being the best on earth, with all the fame and million-dollar contracts that that brings, and flipping burgers, trying to find time to train."

At least that's Kutt's claim. His company, capitalizing on Levine's research and Rusko's engineering, has begun to build something called a Colorado Mountain Room for professional athletes. As part of my preparation for attempting a notorious 20,000-foot peak, I spent two weeks sleeping—or at least trying to—in a room jury-rigged with CAT equipment that simulated oxygen availability at varying altitudes. "No more driving up and down the mountain," promises Kutt. "We turn your bedroom into a nitrogen room—an oxygen-deprived environment in which you can sleep high—train low right in your own home."

I had contacted CAT, one of several U.S. companies now marketing oxygen-deprivation chambers for endurance athletes, at the suggestion of Dr. Peter Hackett, another of America's foremost altitude specialists. Hackett has published extensively on the pathophysiology of altitude-induced illnesses. He summited Everest on a medical research expedition in 1981, directed his own physiology research lab at 14,200 feet on Mount McKinley from 1981 to 1989, and is now president of the International Society for Mountain Medicine. I was interested in discovering whether such a device might be useful in pre-acclimatizing for a speed ascent of a high peak.

"It would be a worthwhile, if limited, experiment," said Hackett. "If you slept in a nitrogen room every night for several weeks prior to departure, even if it doesn't make you climb any faster, it will definitely reduce your risk of AMS, HAPE [high-altitude pulmonary edema], and HACE [high-altitude cerebral edema]."

My wife, Sue, is accustomed to my departures, but not to me leaving before I'm gone. In this case, I quit sleeping with her and moved into the spare bedroom upstairs.

"In the name of science," I said.

"You brave guinea pig you," she said, adding that altitude must have already killed too many brain cells if I was choosing suffering over sex.

Nevertheless, she helped me duct-tape opaque sheets of plastic over the room's windows, closet doorjambs, light fixtures, and electrical outlets.

"Your Mountain Room has to be airtight," said Kutt, "otherwise outside air will leak into the room and you'll never be able to reduce the amount of oxygen."

Once the spare bedroom was swathed in duct tape, two "oxygen concentrators," dishwasher-size machines that separate oxygen from nitrogen, were placed outside the door. Each machine had two hoses that were plugged into the room via holes drilled through the door. One hose sucked out normal air, the other pumped nitrogen-enriched air back in. A computerized control panel with an LED screen that reported the room's oxygen content was bolted onto the inside of the door. Just below it, an eight-inch hole was bored through the door and a ventilation fan installed. Two small oxygen sensors and one carbon dioxide sensor were taped to the walls. An electrical carbon dioxide scrubber—a large metal box filled with a kitty-litter-like gravel that would absorb the excess carbon dioxide I would be exhaling—was set up inside the room.

Because I was the first mountaineer to try out the Mountain Room, and because the computer controlling the machines was a new, untested prototype, Kutt insisted that Hackett determine my altitude protocol, which he did. If everything went smoothly, I was to spend two nights at 10,000 feet, two nights at 12,000 feet, three nights at 14,000 feet, three nights at 16,000 feet, and six nights at 18,000 feet.

The first two nights I set the oxygen meter at 18.69 percent, which translates to 10,000 feet above sea level. Since I already live at 7,200 feet, I slept fine, although the computer-controlled fan kicked on and off erratically, bumping the oxygen level in the room up and down. The third night I staggered in after downing a few too many margaritas, dialed the meter down to 17.3 percent oxygen (12,000 feet), and woke in the middle of the night with nothing less than what I deserved—a screaming headache and a sketchy stomach. But it wasn't all my fault; the computer had again malfunctioned and I was actually up at almost 15,000 feet.

Night four went fine at 12,000 feet, but nights five, six, and seven I slept little. The computer was acting up again, blasting me too high, then dropping me precipitously. To compensate, I started manually overriding the system by simply opening and shutting the door to attain the desired oxygen concentration in the room—a task that meant waking up every hour.

Night eight I should have been at 14.89 percent oxygen—16,000 feet—but I couldn't get above 15,000 feet, and the oxygen concentrators had so overheated that the room was hot as a brothel in Bangkok. Sometime after midnight, I bailed, tiptoeing downstairs and slipping into bed with my wife. ("So, the boy in the bubble returneth!")

Thereafter I missed three nights because my Mountain Room was too hot to sleep in. (Colorado Altitude Training now sells an air-conditioner to supplement its $14,500 setup.)

On night twelve I fell asleep at 10,000 feet and awoke at 17,000 choking for air in a room stiflingly hot. On night thirteen I zoomed from 7,200 feet to 18,200 and had some fine hallucinations. Nights fourteen and fifteen, more heat and more hallucinations. On night sixteen, my last, I shot up to 18,500 feet, got myself good and sick for a few hours, then escaped to sleep with my wife before leaving for the mountain in the morning.

Björn Daehlie, arguably the greatest cross-country skier ever, winner of eight Olympic gold medals, purportedly drives his own oxygen-deprivation RV from race to race—eating, sleeping, and living at moderate altitude, competing at low altitude.

According to Rolf Saeterdal, altitude consultant for the Norwegian Olympic Committee, "Many of Scandinavia's top endurance athletes—runners, cyclists, rowers, cross-country skiers—are using this technology. The Finns have an entire 'nitrogen hotel' where their endurance athletes live. Oxygen is the key element in endurance sports. Controlling it, in both the living and training of athletes, is the future of elite aerobic athletics."

But are oxygen deprivation chambers part of the future of high-altitude mountaineering, notwithstanding my own flawed experiment?

"It's not the increase in the number of red blood cells that is important to a mountaineer," says Hackett, "but rather the pressure of oxygen in these red blood cells, which is primarily a function of breathing harder. Still, it is likely that sleeping or living in a nitrogen chamber for an extended period before going to high altitude will decrease the amount of time it takes to acclimatize in the mountains—the danger is that the technology may be misused by people who have more money than time."

Levine is more circumspect: "If you think of altitude as medicine," he says, "when it comes to pre-acclimatizing for mountains in a nitrogen chamber, we don't yet know what the dose should be or how long it should be administered. Personally, given the option of sleeping in a chamber or climbing in the Alps to pre-acclimatize . . . well, which one would you choose?

"One thing is certain, what determines success or even survival on a mountain isn't usually speed, more often it comes down to good judgment, experience, and common sense—none of which you acquire in a chamber."

So. Did my wifeless, sleep-deprived fortnight of sleeping high and training low make any difference on my climb? Ah, were mountaineering as straightforward as cycling, swimming, or running. The snow was avalanche-prone windslab over blue ice, which forced us to choose a different route, I hadn't slept well for a week because the tent was too small, and my partner and I were as ill-matched as teeth and tinfoil.

McKinley Redux

We hadn't been on the mountain twenty-four hours when it was clear we were incompatible.

Twight bawled for a halt. I peered over my shoulder. He had slumped onto his sled and was glowering at me. I undid my waistbelt and slid off my pack, unhooked myself from the sled, unclipped my harness from the rope, unclipped the rope from the ascenders, unsnapped both feet from my skis, and walked back down the glacier. I stopped whistling and wiped the grin off my face. Already I knew my piping of old rock songs was driving him crazy, my grin an affront.

"I hate, hate, *hate* this!" Twight was vitriolic. Not for the first time, he cursed our "fucking stupidly heavy" sleds and packs and his terrible blisters and our fast pace and . . .

I walked away.

Another team of mountaineers had stopped near us on the trail. They were playing football with a bag of food, stumbling hilariously in their huge boots in the wet snow. I made an interception, tripped, and fell face first, using my head like a shovel. Cheers went up. Lying on my stomach, my face caked with snow, I looked back at Twight. He was still sitting on his sled, hunched and brooding, grim as a stone statue.

I stood up and surveyed the desert of snow ahead. Something in the soft dunes of the glacier looked familiar and I realized I had been here, precisely here, before. Two decades ago, in fact, almost to the day.

The glacier is scalding white, the sun a conflagration. An avalanche booms off a ridge in the distance. Mike Moe, my partner, is caught with his pants down, straddling a crevasse. He leaps to his feet—harness and wool pants and long underwear swaddled around his ankles—pirouettes, throws his arms out, and croons in falsetto:

"The hills are alive/With the sound of music!"

I bullet him with a snowball, triggering a flurry worthy of the wars we waged as kids. A hasty truce is called when two men appear on the horizon. We quickly don our huge packs, hitch ourselves to our ghastly haul bags, and lean into the traces. Minutes later the climbers ski up to us, red plastic sleds wagging like tails behind them. Both men look familiar but I don't know why. The younger one has blond hair, the older black. We ask them what route they climbed.

"West Butt."

"We're heading for the Cassin Ridge," I blurt.

They exchange looks. The stocky, sandy-haired mountaineer nods and says, "Doing it the hard way, I see."

Mike and I don't know what he's talking about. He points to our homemade, 100-pound haul bags.

It is the first day of our first expedition and already we have learned something: our haul bag theory doesn't work. We thought nylon bags would glide along the glacier. They don't. They plow, cutting a foot-deep furrow in the snow, and this only by dint of us straining like draft horses, sweat gushing from our pores.

Perhaps it is our imbecilic, Huck-and-Tom enthusiasm. Perhaps they see in us something of themselves when they were young and inescapably foolish. Perhaps they simply can't stand stupidity in the mountains and feel a duty, as fellow climbers, to keep us from busting a gut.

"Come back to base with us," says the darkly tanned, older alpinist, "and you can have our sleds."

We abandon our bags and ski with them the six or seven miles back to the airstrip on the Southeast Fork of the glacier. Turns out these two had also set out to climb the Cassin, but storms and cold had made it so dangerous they'd taken the trade route up McKinley instead.

At base they empty their kid sleds and give them to us. It's an act of goodwill, a handoff from old partners to young partners. We say thanks, shake hands, and ask their names.

"Yvon Chouinard."

"Rick Ridgway."

Somebody yelled and I arced the food bag back.

Twight was on his feet. We ground onward, two dark spots in a sky-size expanse of ice. We stopped again and again until Twight announced, "Here! We're stopping right here."

We veered off to an abandoned, three-sided snow wall, dug out the drifts, and set up our tent. We were at 10,000 feet, already a day behind schedule, but still intent on a quick ascent of McKinley—a few days acclimatizing on the West Buttress, perhaps a few days sitting out storms, then a three-day push up the Cassin.

The next morning we decided to make a cache to cut weight.

"This is way too much food," said Twight.

"Probably."

"No. This is fucking stupid!"

We had bought the food together. Two hours caroming down the aisles in a Colorado Safeway, pitching whatever either of us wanted into the shopping cart. It was fun. We'd never climbed or hiked or even drank a beer together before that. When the cart was full we figured we had enough. We split the food in the parking lot and parted. I was pleased to see how nonchalant he was about it all. No obsessing. It boded well, I thought. A week later we met in Anchorage at midnight, drove to Talkeetna in the wee hours, and were slowly skiing up the Kahiltna Glacier later that same day.

The food bags were labeled "brkft," "lnch," and "dnnr." Twight muttered, dumped all the bags out in the snow, and started sorting through the pile, one packet of hot chocolate or soup at a time. Two hours later, we still had several heavy bags of food left to take up the mountain—which only made sense given it was just day three of a two-week expedition.

"It's still too much," groaned Twight.

"Fair enough." My patience was dissolving. I grabbed one of the larger bags at random and threw it on the cache.

"What are you doing?" Twight was incredulous.

"Cutting weight."

Twight snatched the bag back. In the end our sleds remained too heavy and Twight started bellyaching ten minutes up the trail. I stopped and told him I was ready to cut all the food. Cut the sleds, cut the packs, cut the rope.

"Let's just take a water bottle, a candy bar, and go for the summit from here." I was serious. I'd done it before. Twight thought I was mad.

Climbing the Cassin had been my idea. I'd asked Mark Twight to be my partner because he was a bold alpinist well known for climbing fast and light, an ascetic philosophy I try to live by. But alpinism and mountaineering are not synonymous. Mountaineering—even if it's only being used as a means to set up for a fast alpine ascent—inevitably entails slogging under heavy loads for numerous days. Twight, as he was so willing to share, abhorred slogging.

I, on the other hand, abhorred whining. Hence, though we may have been matched in philosophy, in temperament we grated on each other like a fork on a china plate.

In many ways a climbing partnership is no different than any other intimate relationship. You sleep side by side, eat from the same pot, piss in the same spot, live cheek-by-jowl day in, day out. It's not enough that your heads be together, your hearts must be as well. Even in the mountains, the fabled redoubt where one wrong step can mean the difference between life and death, technique means less than companionship. And companionship is a matter of chemistry. Mysterious and invisible and effortless. And we didn't have it.

"So what do you say?" I shouted.

Twight said he did not intend to go any faster or lighter than he was going.

"Blackbird singing in the dead of night . . ."

"Take these broken wings and learn to fly . . ."

We're alternating lines, harmonizing on the chorus. In a rare moment of reasonableness, Mike and I have decided that if Chouinard and Ridgway found the Cassin too risky, we probably would too. We're bound for the West Buttress instead. Hammering up the glacier, the rope stays taut between us, like a ligament connecting two bones that form one joint. We move at the same pace. We have always moved at the same pace. We have been partners since boyhood.

In high school we double-dated, built snowcaves, climbed the local crags. After high school we lit out to see the world together. We hitchhiked across North Africa, got arrested in Russia, hopped trains across Europe. When our money ran out we took to sneaking into university cafeterias in Milan, Barcelona, Paris, stealing the uneaten food off the trays of girls too gorgeous to notice two wolfish vagabonds.

Back in the U.S. it was summers in Yosemite or Joshua Tree or the Tetons, winters ice climbing in the Rockies, arguing about Sartre or sex. When we latched on to the idea of climbing McKinley we were penniless college kids clothed by the Salvation Army. We sold T-shirts for funding and sewed all our own equipment: outlandish, ill-fitting jackets, uncomfortable homemade backpacks, Frostline sleeping bags. What we had to buy we bought used. Steel-shanked, fifteen-pound leather double-boots. Garage sale downhill skis with leg-breaker bindings. Useless Salewa ice screws. Miserable, even dangerous, gear. But what we lacked in accoutrements we made up for in a partnership of perfect pitch.

From 10,000 feet, Twight and I sled-hauled to 11,200, made a carry-on up around Windy Corner to the 14,200 camp, then came back down for the night, stashing our skis in the snow at 12,500 just above Squirrel Hill. The next day it was storming, but Twight and I couldn't bear hanging out in the same tent together, so we moved up to 14,200. The day before, both Squirrel Hill and Windy Corner had been so icy we were obliged to strap on our crampons and lug our skis. Thus, when we reached the skis the next day, I suggested we just leave them there. We would only carry them up and then carry them back down—a waste of energy. Twight didn't respond. He just started defiantly loading his boards onto his sled.

"Hey!" I said, shouting into the freezing wind, "we're having a discussion."

"I'm not!" Twight shouted back. "I've decided."

"For yourself, or for the team?" To stay together on the mountain, we had to either both walk, or both ski.

He gave me a quizzical look, as if it had never occurred to him that we were a team, or perhaps even that mountaineering is a team sport.

"Point taken," he screamed, and finished strapping his skis to his sled.

Later that day he shared his lunch with me. It was a peace offering. As we ate in silence, facing different directions, it occurred to me that he wasn't enjoying my company any more than I was enjoying his. This climb was only a warm-up for Twight; in June he planned to attempt an extreme route on McKinley's south face (and would succeed).

I was mulling over our unexpected discordance when, halfway through the morass of crevasses on Windy Corner, it struck me that I didn't have a clue why the notoriously fatalistic Mark Twight climbs. For twenty-five years I had somehow believed that climbers climbed for the same reason that painters painted or writers wrote or composers composed: because they loved it.

How absurdly callow.

The storm attacks out of nowhere. Mike and I have no idea where we are on the mountain. (We're on Windy Corner, the worst possible place to be in a storm.) We dig in immediately, hacking a shallow shelf in the steep slope, hastily surrounding it with blocks of snow and throwing up our A-frame pup tent. We use our ice axes to stake down the fly, but it flaps as violently as a frightened bird.

We tie the two plastic sleds to the ice axes—where they snap horizontally in the wind—and fill the tent with all our gear and dive inside. We have severe frostnip on our hands, fingers, and faces. We huddle close to each other, clamping our hands under our armpits and placing our bare feet against each other's bare bellies. When our hands finally warm up, we press them against the patches of frozen white flesh on each other's faces. After all body parts are thawed, we rewarm our mittens inside our parkas, plug them on, and take up our stations at either end of our flimsy, fair-weather tent. Fearing that the wind is going to tear the tent right off of us, like a tornado lifts away the roof of a cheap house, we hang on to the poles.

The storm intensifies and we are obliged to hold down the tent straight through the night. We tell every dirty joke we know. We swap tall tales, usually about each other, that to us are so funny we double over in laughter.

There were perhaps 100 climbers camped at 14,200 in late May—a multinational village of Czechs, Swedes, Slavs, Canadians, Welsh, Americans, French, Brits, Aussies, and Japanese. A few 8,000-meter summiters, many solid mountaineers, some hikers who had never worn crampons—and the mountain brought us all to our knees. It was viciously cold. The cold stripped us, easily and quickly, of our pretensions and destroyed any hierarchy, real or ego-induced. Every last one of us was just hoping to summit via the easiest path possible and get down alive.

Once again, as it had twenty years earlier, the mountain called the shots. The intense cold made the Cassin, a finesse route that could require technical rock climbing in thin gloves, out of the question. Twight and I briefly considered the West Rib or the Messner Couloir, but both had two feet of avalanche-prone windslab over blue ice. We made three fast—sub-three-hour—acclimatization climbs up to 17,300, unroped and barely together. Twight borrowed a spare tent from a fellow climber so we no longer had to share our little icebox. We weren't a team anymore. I awoke early and cooked breakfast; Twight cooked dinner wearing headphones. I spent our rest days wandering around camp talking with other climbers. Twight hung out at the Park Service rescue station or holed up in his tent.

One night around the camp stove I asked him what he was thinking.

"About when this trip will be over," he barked.

After hunkering down for two days on Windy Corner, Mike and I push on. Camp 14,200 is buried under four feet of snow, the few tents there crushed. We excavate a pit, put our tent down inside, build snowwalls, and start winter camping for a few days.

"You know, Marco," Mike says one fine morning, "it was only forty below last night."

"Man, home's colder!"

It almost was. During the winter, to prepare for McKinley, we had skied into Rocky Mountain National Park each time an Arctic storm blew down, winter-camped for a week, and fought our way up frozen waterfalls. We both read Minus 148: *The Winter Ascent of Mt. McKinley*, by Art Davidson, and considered the title's temperature our benchmark for when suffering should begin. Above that, we figured, it's all good times.

The day we plan to move up to 16,000, Mike isn't feeling so hot. Headache, nausea. I make a solo carry of food and fuel up to our stash on the ridge—we're still motivated to summit. By the time I get back down, Mike is sick. Mortally sick. His face and hands are bloated, his breathing quick and bubbly, his movements simultaneously sluggish and jerky. We both realize—and will later confirm—that he has pulmonary *and* cerebral edema. We pack up and descend immediately, hoping to get down to 8,000 feet by midnight. We don't make it. Another storm pounces less than an hour after we leave and we're forced to hide out in a collapsed igloo at 11,000 feet. The storm pins us down like a lion with its paw on the head of a gazelle. For four days we can't even crawl out to relieve ourselves. We sing every song we know, trying to out-howl the roar of the storm.

"Rocky Raccoon . . ."

"Checked into his room . . ."

"Only to find Gideon's Bible . . ."

Mike's condition doesn't improve, but it doesn't worsen, and that is enough. We both know our grand, inaugural expedition is over. But no sweat, we've already planned the next one.

Twight and I summited, but not with each other.

We'd met two eager lads from Dartmouth, Bart and Fred. They were the same age as I was when I first came to Mount McKinley. They too had dreams of doing the Cassin Ridge (and a month later would fulfill them) but, like everyone else at Camp 14,200 at that time, they were bent on climbing the West Buttress.

Whenever Bart and Fred were around, Twight seemed transformed. He became animated and voluble; he even smiled. Nothing
close to the guy I'd been climbing with. Fred, in particular, was
starstruck. He'd read Twight's recent dark manifesto and was thrilled
to meet the guru in person. Twight responded warmly.

One morning we set out for the summit as a foursome. But at
17,000, Bart started slowing down. He was clearly suffering from
inadequate acclimatization, couldn't catch his breath, and thus
couldn't keep up. His partner, Fred, raced ahead with Twight. I
dropped back and took up with Bart. Together, we moved steadily. I
found myself thinking about Mike. About how, if things had been different, we would have been up here together. About all the expeditions we eventually did together. About how as a young man I had
known instinctively, without a shred of doubt, that it was the partnership, not the peak, that mattered.

It was minus thirty-seven the morning we set out and minus
thirty-nine the evening we came down. Twight and Fred went from
14,200 to the 20,320-foot summit and back down in ten hours; Bart
and I, discussing family and friendship along the way, did it in eleven.

On the summit, lumpy clouds had rolled in making the highest
mountain in North America appear to be just another nondescript
bump of white. Bart and I hugged each other, took perfunctory photos, and then just stood there for a few minutes, staring out into the
gauzy emptiness.

KIN

Pulling Your Weight

I have a pull-up bar in the furnace room of my basement. I mounted it between two joists the day we moved in. We were sleeping on the floor in the dining room and would be for two months—the house was a wreck and we were fixing it up one room at a time—but the bar was important.

When work is going well, I go downstairs at five in the morning. It is dark. The furnace breathes like a slumbering octopus; the water heater gurgles. I am in my underwear, still swathed in the warmth of bed and another body, although the concrete is cold against the soles of my feet. I take off my wedding band and my watch and place them on the workbench opposite the furnace.

Sometimes there is pale starlight slanting through the basement windows, cutting my body in half. I stand on my tiptoes and grasp the bar. Long ago I wound it with athletic tape for a better grip. The white tape is badly discolored now, and worn through in places. I hold on to the bar and lift my feet off the concrete. I hang there for a moment, stretched out, then pull up.

My head rises up into the space between the two-by-twelves. They support the main floor of our house, the bedrooms in which my wife and two daughters are sleeping. The joists were set in 1916, when good houses were built on solid foundations with clean, full-dimension lumber. Two inches was still two inches, a foot a foot. A craftsman built our house. All the door frames are still square, the walls plumb, the double-hung windows still glide up and down.

I pull up, my chin slips over the bar, then I uncrank back down to a dead hang. I do twenty pull-ups and drop off, shake it out. After three sets, I crack my neck, go to my office, flip on my computer, sit down, and with luck, start to write.

Pull-ups are a tradition in my family. A rite among the four brothers. Me, Steve, Dan, Christopher, in descending age. Before my brother Steve got divorced, he had his pull-up bar in the basement as well. Later, in the shabby apartment, he ran it across the width of his closet and tacked up a couple pinups for inspiration. Now he has his own house again, and his pull-up bar is back in the basement. Between the joists in his furnace room, just like mine.

Dan doesn't have a pull-up bar at home. He doesn't need one. He owns a gymnastics club. He does his pull-ups on the high bar late at night, after he's finished coaching all the little kids who want to be what he once was.

Christopher is the youngest. I think he had a pull-up bar in most of his apartments. Or at least one in all his girlfriends' apartments. Being the youngest, he is of course the most laid-back. He's in Chile now, "painting murals and dancing salsa with the most beautiful women on earth." But I bet, when no one's watching, he's snapping out a few pull-ups at four in the morning in some empty, moonlit playground.

Our tradition, this thing between four brothers, began back in junior high. Junior high is where boys learn to hate. Steve went out for football and got his arm broken during the first game. The coach came off the sidelines baying and cursing and wiggled it and said it was just fine, and Steve played the rest of the season with it like that. Winter came, and I went out for wrestling and broke a guy's arm accidentally and felt awful because they had to rush him to the hospital for surgery. The same coach barked, "What's your fuckin' problem, boy? You won the match!"

That year a gymnastics club started up in town and saved us. It was above an old auto parts store. A few ratty mats, a colossal leather pommel horse, some rings slung from the rafters on canvas webbing. I quit the wrestling team, Steve forswore football, and we joined

together. There were lots of girls, but we were the only boys besides
an odd kid named Robin whose dad was a sculptor. We took to it like
monkeys. Soon we were swinging joyfully through the air, tumbling
madly if badly, walking on our hands up the stairs.

But gymnastics was an alien concept in Wyoming, incomprehensible to most of its residents. There was no opponent. In real sports,
there were two sides, and they brawled until somebody won. That's
the way football worked, and basketball and wrestling and rodeos,
even hunting. Those were the sports people understood and
respected.

When the junior high football coach discovered we had quit real
sports for gymnastics, he was apoplectic. He called us a couple of
pussies. Pansies. Girlies. He shouted it in the hallway whenever he saw
us, his arms crossed against his chest to show off his biceps. This
inspired the wrestlers and football players. They took to sucker-
punching us any chance they got. Dad told us to let other guys pick
the fights, but that we'd better finish them. Something we couldn't do.

Partly in hopes of retribution, but mostly because we needed
more strength to do the difficult strength moves in gymnastics—an
iron cross on the rings for instance—Steve and I bicycled down to
Midwest Sports, a cavernous warehouse beside the railroad tracks. It
supplied uniforms for team sports. We found what we were looking
for on a shelf amid chin straps and mouth guards. EXTENDABLE CHIN-UP
BAR was printed on the box, and FOR GENERAL FITNESS AND PLEASURE. It
cost five dollars. We took it down into the basement, where our bedroom was, and bolted it to the bathroom doorjambs. We made a secret pact: no going in or out of the bathroom—to piss, crap, brush
teeth, anything—without doing ten pull-ups. We even made a little
sign on an index card and tacked it above the light switch: TEN PULL-
UPS, PLEASE! We were in junior high.

After about a year, when there was no other option, we started
accomplishing what Dad expected. Another year and pull-ups had
become a part of life. We didn't even notice that our admonition had

disappeared. We did pull-ups before breakfast and before bed, straight through high school.

When Steve and I went off to college, we left the pull-up bar behind for Dan and Christopher. Their bedroom was next to ours in the basement. They were in gymnastics now. Dan was starting to get shoulders, but Christopher was still a noodle. A new version of our index card reappeared on the bathroom wall.

I switched from gymnastics to rock climbing in college, a sport for which you can never do enough pull-ups. I climbed with an upperclassman built like an Irish boxer in both body and mind. He was a notorious, indefatigable crack climber. He immediately began dragging me up routes that were far above my head. He lived in a one-room garage with the back wall falling off and told me he did 400 pull-ups a day on the crack in the ceiling.

I was now doing pull-ups on the bedroom doorjamb of my girl-friend's apartment. After sex, when she was asleep and I was wide-awake. Before we went cowboy dancing when I was dressed and in my boots and she was putting on her makeup. Steve was with an Iran-ian girl living in a condemned building downtown for forty bucks a month. He did his pull-ups on a dripping water pipe.

By graduate school I was doing at least one, usually two expedi-tions a year. I did pull-ups in the hotel rooms in Hong Kong, New Delhi, Nairobi, La Paz. I did pull-ups hanging off trains rumbling across China or Bolivia or Burma. I did pull-ups on the boulders at base camp.

After graduate school, when my wife and I were living apart and I was trying to master my craft, wherever I was, I'd nail up a length of pipe or PVC. When I was on assignment out of the country, I did pull-ups on any clothesline pole or tree limb or brothel shower rod or even the wainscoting in a bar.

Eventually we bought a house and started living together like husband and wife. It is an old, spacious place with seven bedrooms, leaded glass, and maple floors. I could have put the pull-up bar any-where. But I hung it in the basement, where it belongs.

My study is also in the basement. A writer works in his head so the need for big windows and a pretty view has always escaped me. When work is going poorly, I walk back to the shop and knock out a few pull-ups. Then again, when the writing is going well, through sheer exuberance I'll do a few pull-ups.

Steve used to work for a large firm in a high rise, wearing a suit and tie, so at that time he had to do them in the corporate gym. Now he works for himself. His office is in his basement as well. Perhaps we become what we were.

I can imagine that there are times, maybe nine-thirty in the morning, maybe right after lunch, when we're doing pull-ups at the same moment. Maybe all four of us are doing pull-ups at the same time, thousands of miles apart. Chris, setting aside his paintbrush and popping off a few in his studio in Concepción. Dan pulling so hard he bounces the slim horizontal bar in his gym.

You seldom see anyone in a weight room on the pull-up bar. Pull-ups are too hard. They aren't like push-ups. With push-ups half your weight is still on your feet. And they aren't anything like most of the arm exercises you can do with machines, where all your weight is on your ass. All those machines are just crutches. They're designed to make working out easier. Massive muscles mean nothing. The only real measure of strength is in contrast to your weight.

To do a pull-up, you must lift the entire weight of your body off the ground. It is as if you have raised your arms in jubilation and then must bring your body up with your spirit. It is an angelic act, a stren-uous act. It goes against gravity. Against the will of the earth.

Because pull-ups are difficult, over the years, it's easy to get lazy. Easy to get heavy. Life and beer and kids conspire. Thus, sometime after college, the four of us started a little contest.

It's held around Christmas. Since we live far apart, it's difficult to get together every winter, but we've managed it most years. It is a ritual. In autumn we start calling one another at odd hours, leaving cryptic, adolescent messages: "Doing sets of twenty-five" or "You die this year, bro." Of course when we actually talk, we claim we've got a beer gut or a bad shoulder or no time to exercise. But we all have our bar.

The contest is held at the folks' house. There is no preordained day or time. Usually the event takes place in the evening. We start razzing one another and wrestling and getting off shoulder punches— like the lances a picador drives into the shoulders of the bull. Pretty soon it's time for the test.

Dad is the judge. He takes four matchsticks, breaks them off at different lengths, and holds them before us clamped in his fist. We each point to one. This is how the order of the competitors is determined, but he doesn't tell us what position we have drawn. To go first is always best; get it over with. To go last is always worst.

Dad then descends into the basement with a couple cold beers. He puts a chair just outside the doorway of his shop and sits down among his tools. There is a wooden pull-up bar in the doorjamb.

The four of us wait pensively in the living room. We feel like we did before a big gymnastics meet two decades ago. Butterflies, self-doubt. But we are adults. Half of us have children.

Mom stands at the top of the stairs and Dad shouts up the name of the first competitor. We have all gone first. We have all gone last. When your name is called, you descend into the basement and strip down to your skivvies.

You can do whatever you want to warm up. Clap push-ups, jumping jacks, run in little circles like a nervous boxer. You can take as long as you want. Dad is in no hurry.

You can do either overhand or underhand pull-ups, your choice. But once you touch the bar, your effort has begun. You must start from a dead hang, arms straight, feet dangling. On every pull-up your chin must extend decisively over the bar, otherwise it is not counted.

You must return to a dead hang after each pull-up, otherwise it is not counted. You can rest between pull-ups all you want, but your feet cannot touch the ground.

By the time you begin, you are in a lather. Adrenaline is coursing through your body. But you have to control it. You have to be careful not to do the first ten or fifteen too fast, or your arms will grind to a halt. Lactic acid. It's like suddenly having sludge in your veins. The trick is to use the same rhythm you use at home on your own bar. Do them like you do there. No one watching. Just you rising up and down, steady as a piston in the dark.

Of course, the last few are impossible. Your arms are like slabs of lead, your body heavy as a dead man's. You want to give up. Fuck it. But you don't know how many everyone else will do. Sometimes, when you finally drop off, you collapse. Dad does not tell you how many you have done.

Usually you are shaking from the ordeal, and it is difficult to put your clothes back on. When you come up from the basement, you are pale and nauseous. Mom and our sisters and our wives or girlfriends are all aghast, repulsed by this pointless show of machismo.

After all four of us have had our turn, Dad sits in the basement and finishes his beer, then comes up and makes the announcement. He calls your name and your number, nothing more.

We have all won and we have all lost. As we get older, some years are better than others. But there are no excuses. What you have done to yourself in the last year is your own problem. You are expected to pull your own weight.

The Snowcave

This is the way we imagined it, Mike Moe and I. Our kids in the mountains together, just as we were when we were kids. We talked about it whenever we were too far from home, on expeditions, lying on our backs in the tent when we should have been letting our bodies sleep.

Justin refuses to wear his backpack on his shoulders. It's heavy because he brought his dinosaur books. He lets the straps slip down to his elbows, binding his arms, so when he trips he falls face first. He doesn't mind. It gives him a chance to examine the bugs on the snow. Addi has her teddy bear and two other stuffed animals in her pack. Addi and Justin are both in snowsuits, knit caps that keep falling off, mittens already soaked. They're skiing, slowly, across Lake Marie. They are both six years old, born a month apart. They are the same height. They have the same red faces, the same easy laugh, the same unquenchable curiosity. Justin collects insects, Addi collects rocks.

It is June in Wyoming at 10,000 feet. The snow is eight feet deep, the lakes still frozen. We are skiing together to the snowcave. We're going winter camping, an endeavor best done in summer—double the sunlight, triple the temperature. The snowcave is carved from the same drift Mike and I built caves in when we were boys. Of course it's not the identical drift but a descendant. A deep, beautiful drift in a long line of deep, beautiful drifts. Hidden in the lee of a glacial erratic the size of an apartment building, it took us years to find it.

When we get to the snowcave Justin and Addi can't get their skis off fast enough. They drop their packs and creep inside as if it were a tunnel into another world. The ceiling is over four feet high, which means they can stand up. They run their fingers along the chiseled walls and scuff the ice floor with their boots. Addi lies down, checking out the levelness of the sleeping platform. Justin discovers the air hole and sticks his arm up inside it. In the next two days the snowcave will be a secret hideout, a fortress, a bear's den, a spaceship.

We were older when Mike and I built our first snowcave but the enchantment was the same. It was a fort to us too, a hand-hewn refuge in the wilderness. Over the course of two decades we built all kinds of snowcaves. Miserable holes no self-respecting marmot would inhabit, circular lairs with sensual candlelighting that inspired carnal speculations, burrows so far below the surface that snowmobiles roared over our roof without us knowing. One year, with the help of our younger brothers, we mined a cavern so expansive we played croquet. Upside-down ice axes for mallets, bound wool socks for balls. Five days later the ceiling had sagged so far we had to use the ice axes as stanchions to hold it up.

When we were young and literal we believed winter camping was properly done in winter. Once, in high school, we set out in the dead of January in the coldest storm in a generation. Mike and I thought this good sport. In town it got down to fifty-four below zero. We were thousands of feet higher and the wind was furious. Maybe it got down to absolute zero. Who knows. We were having too good a time to notice, snug as bugs in a rug in our snowcave. We brought enough food for an expedition and decided to stay a few extra days. By the time we got back home our terrified families—traditionally stoic and optimistic about our misadventures—were mounting a rescue.

Not to romanticize snowcaves. They're too hard to build correctly and take too much time and energy. Nine out of ten times a tent is better. But that's not the point. Never was. We had tents even back then but what fun would that have been? A snowcave was the opportunity to build something. A chance to dig and crawl on your belly and get cold and wet. A chance to battle the elements, wield mortal weapons, prove how we could beat the odds no matter what they were. What more could Wyoming boys want?

At dusk, clouds fat as pregnant salmon swim through a darkling sky and Justin begins to howl. He cranes his head back and lets her rip. Addi joins in and they howl and then break into ordinary screaming. Trying to one-up each other, they scream until their youthful throats grow rough. I don't stop them. If you can't scream your head off in the mountains, where can you? It's something I learned from Mike. He didn't worship mountains. Only people who've never spent much time in the mountains worship them. Like guys who never go on a date worship women. Live or work in the high country and you have to be more practical than that.

When the moon slips out Addi and Justin insist on a ghost story. We are at the base of a black, thousand-foot wall of quartzite. It's called the Diamond. Mike and I used to attempt to climb it every winter, never succeeding. The cornices on the ridge have been breaking off all day—rumbling down the couloirs, leaving piles of debris that look small and benign until you ski up to them and discover the blocks are bigger than trucks. I tell them that actually avalanches are started by ghosts. You can't see them, but they're up there, jumping up and down on the cornices, laughing.

"How did they get up there?" asks Justin.

"They climbed," I say.

"Ghosts are climbers," states Addi, as if it were obvious.

"And skiers," says Justin.

After kicking off a few avalanches the ghosts get the idea that it would be fun to slide down on one, so they do. They ride the avalanches like cowboys ride bulls. One arm waving in the air.

The ghosts slide right down the mountain into the lake, which is half-thawed.

"Right into the water!" shouts Justin, delighted.

"They like the cold because they don't get cold," explains Addi. "They're ghosts."

The story goes along, growing more and more complex, with lots of ad hoc events. It starts to get late.

At this point the ghosts discover two young snowcavers at the base of the mountain and naturally manage to lure them out into the dark. (Addi and Justin peer up at the dark massif overhead.) The ghosts want the two junior adventurers to come with them, into the everlasting unknown, but they are scared. They don't want to go. The ghosts start to pull on the children.

"I'm tired," says Addi.

"Me too," adds Justin quickly.

They unanimously decide to hurry into the snowcave and scooch down into their sleeping bags.

Before crawling in for the night I force both of them to relieve themselves, but it doesn't help. Too many cups of tomato soup and hot chocolate. Justin awakes at two A.M. To keep him from soiling or soaking his longjohns, I make him strip off his underwear and crawl bare-assed out of the snowcave. He stands in the snow, alone in the moonlight with the clouds flying by like ghosts. Shooting back inside, he dives into his bag and is instantly sound asleep. Addi wakes at three and I make her do the same thing. Beyond the cave entrance I can see her squatting, staring warily up at the night sky.

In the morning I have a plan. I want us to climb Medicine Bow peak. I want them to want to climb Medicine Bow peak. They aren't interested. They want to go sledding. I remove the duffel bags and nylon straps from the haul sleds and they revert back to what they were originally—five-dollar Kmart kid sleds. Justin and Addi make only a few runs before wandering off to a newly exposed creek. The creek winds back and forth around drifts before disembouching into Lake Marie. The lake is entirely frozen except for a thin strip along the northern shore where this creek enters it. A scatter of angular rocks protrude from the glacial waters. It looks like a scene from the South Pole. We christen our discovery "Little Antarctica."

Addi and Justin begin hopping stone to stone above the icy water, first tentatively, then with growing boldness. At first they pretend they are penguins. Then decide they don't like penguins. "Penguins are birds that can't fly," says Justin. He says he would rather be an Alaskan wolf and Addi thinks she would rather be an Eskimo girl fishing through holes in the ice. They both instinctively throw rock after rock into the slice of open water, fascinated by the blue-black liquid. Water is magic to children, the only substance they encounter in life that can be played with endlessly and never broken. Water will always go back to being what it was before they dropped it or stepped on it.

The water, although frigid, is only several feet deep. I admonish them not to fall in, then tramp back up to the snowcave to do chores. That's right. I leave two six-year-olds on the edge of a freezing lake in the middle of the mountains, alone.

Still, I pop my head out of the snowcave to check on them more often than I should. They are a ways off. I observe that Addi has a bit more balance than Justin—but more telling, is fearful of getting wet. She bounds above the water with concentration and precision. Justin on the other hand revels in being off balance. After watching him slip off the rocks several times, his legs sinking up to his thighs in the ice-cold water before he drags himself out, I realize he's not slipping at all. He's doing it intentionally, just to see what will happen. From this distance I can't make out his mischievous grin, but I recognize it.

Ten years earlier on the edge of Lake Marie. It is just after dawn. We are on our way to scale the Diamond.

"Your muscles will freeze before you make it across," I say.

"Bet they won't," counters Mike.

"Freeze solid and you'll sink like a rock!"

Mike scoffs.

"Wanna bet?"

"Burrito dinner."

We shake on it. Mike strips in ten seconds and wades into the lake bellowing homemade obscenities. When the water is up to his balls he dives in and begins swimming ferociously. The iceberg is floating in the middle of the lake, perhaps 200 yards from shore. The snow around the lake is still three feet deep. July in the mountains of Wyoming. He plows out to the ice block like a seal in the Arctic Ocean. Next thing I know he has hauled himself up onto the iceberg and is dancing around on top, barefoot and buck-naked. Then he dives off and swims briskly back to shore. When he comes out of the gelid water, stomping footprints in the snow, his body is a bluish pink. He tries to give me his I-told-you-so smirk but the muscles in his face won't budge.

It takes Mike two full hours and 500 feet of climbing to warm up.

Mike was the only man I knew who was an honest-to-God empiricist. He insisted on trying everything himself, as if it were impossible to learn anything except through firsthand experience. We were both like this; it was the genesis of our friendship. We inspired each other. Acts of profound stupidity were commonplace. Knowledge was to be gained by trial and error—not by listening to somebody tell us how or why or when we should or could or shouldn't or couldn't. When it came to the outdoors, we rarely consulted books. We were hell-bent on reinventing the wheel. We became self-taught outdoorsmen. We taught ourselves how to ski, how to climb, how to backpack, how to build snowcaves. And for that reason it took us a long time to get good. Without instructors you learn very slowly. You make a lot of mistakes. What you're really learning is not the craft you're practicing. What are you learning?

You only realize it years afterward. Independence. Resourceful-
ness. Equanimity.

Later in the day Addi, Justin, and I follow coyote tracks across the
flank of the mountain. They are at least twelve hours old but Addi and
Justin don't know that. The wily coyote could be behind the next
boulder. They both want to know why all the trees are so short and
look like flags, branches growing only on one side. I teach them the
word "krummholz" and try to explain the savagery of the wind,
recounting another Mike-and-Mark adventure when both of us were
right here, wearing huge winter-climbing packs, and were lifted
straight up off the ground.

Throughout the day I make them carry their own backpacks with
their own water bottles and snacks. I make them rub the snot off their
faces with the back of their mittens. I show them how to wipe with
snow instead of toilet paper, which leads to a hair-and-all discussion
of alpine scatology.

In the afternoon we build a snowman and have a snowball fight.
By then their snowsuits are soaked through and they're beginning to
shiver. The wind has begun and bruised clouds are rolling overhead.

As I reload the sleds it begins to snow. We start the slow ski out
to the car. Addi is the leader. She insists that her hands are not cold
and that she doesn't have to put her gloves back on. Fine. Justin insists
that his head is not cold and that he doesn't have to wear his wool cap.
Fine.

We contour around the open water and head out over the frozen
lake. As we shuffle along I try to get Justin to pull his pack up onto his
shoulders but he insists on letting it fall down to his elbows and bang
him on the back of the legs. For a moment I almost get angry. Then,
suddenly, I laugh out loud. I throw my head back and look up into the
moving sky and laugh. Justin skis up beside me.

"Watcha doing?"

I look over my shoulder at our ski tracks cutting onto the lake. I look ahead at Addi heading into the trackless snow. Justin is only six. I could make something up, but I don't.

"This is where we spread your dad's ashes. Do you remember?"

Justin is excited. "We're skiing on my dad's ashes?"

I nod.

Somehow this seems wonderful to Justin, as if he were once again riding on Mike's shoulders.

Mike Moe, Dan Moe, Sharon Kava, and Brad Humphrey died on an expedition to the Arctic on September 1, 1995.

A Mere Flesh Wound

In the fight between you and the world,
back the world.

—Franz Kafka

I am wearing a corset. Neo-medieval armor with wide Velcro straps
hidden beneath my shirt. It squeezes me together, immobilizing my rib
cage. It's supposed to give my ribs a chance to weld themselves back together, but I don't think it's doing much. I'll be taking it off soon.

So what happened? What's the story?

I slipped, that's all. My feet shot out from under me and I fell. I
was a thousand feet off the ground on the face of a mountain in the
dead of winter. My partner and I had skied in and gotten halfway up
the wall before the storm hit. Within minutes waterfalls of snow were
pouring over us. I was leading. One ice axe buried in the ice, one flailing like a Viking battle-axe, both crampons stabbed onto tiny toe-
holds. When my feet slid out the full weight of my body and
backpack dropped onto one arm.

I heard the pop. Sounded like a boy plucking his mouth with his
finger. Forced a scream out of me. I knew what it was immediately.
My eighth or ninth rib, probably both, had torn away from the carti-
lage, just like you tear a bone from a boiled chicken.

So now I'm in this straitjacket. I can only take shallow breaths.
Coughing is ridiculous, sneezing out of the question. If I make the
wrong move, a few volts shoot through me like a dog with a shock
collar. I can't run, can't bike, can't sleep at night. Just as I'm drifting

off, I'll inadvertently roll over and my bones will dislodge and I'll yelp. For the time being, my wife, Sue, is sleeping in the guest room.

My mom called practically the minute I got back from the mountain. She is clairvoyant, like all moms. She asked the same things Sue asked. Was I all right? Did I have X-rays? What did the doctor say?

Then my dad got on the line.

"Same thing happened to me a few years back. Remember."

Actually it was a few decades back. Dad and I were wrestling and it got out of hand. Mom was yelling at us to take the roughhousing outside but it was too late. We'd already lifted each other off the ground in a bear hug and thrown ourselves over the kitchen table.

The doc gave Dad a "step-in," a girdle. He was abashed. Mom said it served him right. Which is exactly what Sue said when she found out that we hadn't stopped climbing when I got hurt, but kept going for several more hours to the summit.

The brace restricts movement so it's difficult to lift my daughters. The youngest doesn't notice a difference but the oldest knows I am hurt and therefore won't let me pick her up. I tell her that Mommy is exaggerating but she won't believe me. Three years old and already she sees straight through machismo.

Steve and Dan, two of my three brothers, were in town last weekend. Dan had recently taken a fall himself. He was up on the roof of his half-rotten Victorian house, after midnight, trying to fix something when a board snapped. He fell twenty feet and is in finer shape than I: a concussion, two broken ribs in his back, and a broken wrist.

For old times' sake we rented Monty Python and the Holy Grail and howled through the whole thing. The favorite scene:

King Arthur is trotting through Sherwood Forest in search of brave and noble men who will join his Knights of Camelot. From a distance he watches two knights battle, the black knight eventually skewering the gray knight through the slit in his helmet. Blood spurts out as if from a hose. (We roar.)

King Arthur reins up, praises the Black Knight, and invites him to become a Knight of the Round Table. The Black Knight, like all courageous men of the silver screen, is silent. King Arthur tries to cajole him into joining but the Black Knight won't budge. So, of course, they get into a fight.

King Arthur is the better swordsman for he has the magic sword. In one swing he severs the Black Knight's arm off at the shoulder. Blood squirts out.

"'Tis but a scratch!" shouts the Black Knight.

King Arthur lops off the other arm. Blood spurts everywhere. The Black Knight, now entirely unarmed, cries, "A mere flesh wound!" (We crow.)

King Arthur, incredulous, slices off one of the Black Knight's legs but the Black Knight is indomitable. He keeps coming. He hops straight at King Arthur and tries to head-butt him with his helmet.

"You're mad!" shouts King Arthur, and with that lops off his remaining leg. King Arthur then continues on his way in search of brave men while the Black Knight, insulted and apoplectic, shouts: "You yellow bastard! Come back and get what's coming to you! I'll bite your leg off!"

(We fall off the couch.)

After the movie the three of us sat around the kitchen table drinking beer.

"Isn't that the same wrist?" said Steve, thumping Dan's cast.

Dan grinned. Years ago, in gymnastics, he broke his wrist several times. Now he's a gymnastics coach.

Steve pondered his arm with its twisted, thickened wrist. "Remember ice skating?" he said.

Back when we were boys Dad tried to teach me and Steve how to ice-skate backward. He was sweeping around the rink in graceful circles, scissoring his legs. It was brilliant. Then some hotshot kid clipped him. The tumble snapped his wrist.

"In the wrist department, Christopher still wins," I said.

Christopher is our youngest brother. It was at a party. Things got out of hand and somehow Christopher ended up diving out the window. Which, since he was also once a gymnast, would have been just fine—land on your hands, tuck your head, roll out. But it was a second-story window. Broke both wrists.

"What about you!" cried Dan.

He stood up, and, holding his bad arm with his good arm, told the story: Dan and I and Christopher were on a bicycle ride across Africa. One day my front wheel hit a rock and I flipped onto my face. I managed to slow my fall by getting my arm out and rolling on my shoulder, but it knocked me out cold nonetheless. Woke up with a busted hand and a broken cheek.

"Your head sounded like a pumpkin when it hit the pavement."

"You don't have any room to talk," I said.

A thousand miles earlier, on that same bike ride, we were benighted just before reaching a high pass in the Atlas Mountains of Morocco. It was pitch black. Dan stepped off the side of the road to relieve himself, and fell off a cliff.

"You're the only guy I know who's broken his leg taking a piss."

This goes on for hours. Broken bones, torn ligaments, popped tendons.

The last time I had this kind of body harness was when I broke my collarbone. The neighbor boy and I were tussling on top of a fence and he threw me off. I remember my pals were impressed that I could get hurt just falling off a fence.

Generally speaking, a broken appendage is a pretty lucky break for a boy. Provides you with instant stature. Makes you a card-carrying, dues-paying rowdy. Some of my friends fell off fences all the time and never managed to break a bone.

For a boy, the first time you hurt yourself is often the first time you really take note of your body. Before that—and quickly resumed thereafter—you've spent every waking moment cruising around, acting wild, not even noticing the vehicle you're in. An injury forces you to make acquaintance with your corporeal self. It is the beginning of a long, periodic education in human physiology. Every time you get hurt you learn something new. Which bones are which—humerus, radius, ulna, femur. Which muscles are which—biceps, deltoids, lats, traps, abs. What ligaments are and how tendons work. After a decade you know your insides pretty well. After several decades you believe you can accurately self-diagnose. You know more than the doctor so you don't need to see one.

Injuries also play a positive role in a man's emotional education. Three things happen when a guy gets hurt. First, he is forced to step back for a minute. This precipitates reflection, which often leads to a temporary recognition of mortality—something he is loath to do any other day of the week. Second, getting hurt helps him empathize with his fellow man—another virtue. (Didn't Dostoyevsky say suffering is the origin of consciousness.) Third, sustaining a self-inflicted wound ensures kudos from his pals. The way the guys look at it, he got close and didn't get killed. He slipped on the tightrope of life and caught himself. It's as if life were this grand obstacle course with snake pits and lions' dens and quicksand and by God he pulled himself through another one. They're proud of him. That's why they give him abuse. Giving a guy abuse helps him avoid self-pity—something some of us are as wont to roll in as dogs are to roll in shit. The more abuse, the bigger the story. The bigger the story, the more abuse.

Guys wonder about guys who don't get any abuse. Something's wrong. And they really wonder about guys who've never broken anything. What've they been doing their whole lives? (Of course none of this applies to getting sick. Sickness is a disgraceful, ignoble condition that turns many a man back into a little boy.)

In between injuries most men treat their bodies like machines. Keep the gas tank full. Check the oil now and then. Rotate tires. If it ain't broke don't fix it.

But, sooner or later, something always breaks. Then you have to get scoped for a torn ACL or MCL, lay off for a couple weeks because of a compression fracture, wear a sling to heal a rotator cuff, take pills for tendinitis. These are the kinds of injuries you get doing something. Shooting hoops. Running bases. Roofing. Riding. Kicking. Gliding. These are the kinds of injuries young men brag about.

Old men talk about other injuries, internal hitches. Hemorrhoids. Root canals. Colon cancer. Mendacious maladies they feel they didn't do anything to deserve. That's what pisses them off, makes them ashamed. At the very least they could have been having some fun when something broke, instead of just slipping on the stairs. Alas, these are the injuries you get from having survived all the injuries you got from doing all the things you once did.

Young men don't like to hear about these kinds of injuries. They hang on to the myth of immortality as long as they can. Like Michael Jordan floating above the rim. Like a perfect spiral suspended in air. The old guys encourage it. They know what happens when your feet finally touch down. You get hit. Hard. Young men want to die doing a layup or crossing the finish line or climbing a mountain. Something valiant and bold. Not just going on until the going itself gets you. Nothing heroic about that. Right?

I'm taking this corset off now. I'm healed. I'll give it back to Dad. He's wrestling with the grandkids now.

I never went to the doc. I did call a buddy who is an emergency room MD. When I told him my story, he laughed, said there wasn't much I could do for it anyway, then launched into a great yarn about how he broke his ribs kayaking.

He Ain't Heavy

"Brothers are you? All four."

We nod and Steve Woodford's hawklike head pivots, looking at each of us.

"Well, mates," he says, in a jaunty South African accent, "this is a simple sport: do it right, you live—do it wrong, you don't."

He holds back a grin.

"Equipment failures occur, but they're not the primary cause of bouncing. Pilot error is what kills people. Panic."

Woodford would know. He's jumped out of a plane 7,824 times, pulling his reserve chute on seven occasions. He is a professional skydiving instructor. He was in South Africa's Airborne Special Forces and operated behind enemy lines in Angola. He's won medals at national skydiving competitions and holds several skydiving records. With a tan, lined face and taut body—he's the paradigm of an ex-paratrooper.

Woodford slots in an ancient-looking video, and we watch as a man at a brown desk in a brown suit with a ZZ Top beard tells us that there is one death for every 46,500 jumps and that if we have any doubts whatsoever about what we are about to undertake, it is our grave responsibility to reconsider. Naturally we've already signed the initial-at-a-hundred-places waiver: *I understand the scope, nature, and extent of risks involved in parachuting . . . I understand that parachuting is a dangerous activity in which there is substantial risk of injury and death . . . I expressly and voluntarily assume all risk of death or personal injury . . .*

"Enough of that nonsense," says Woodford, ejecting the video and dropping a parachute pack onto the table. "Let's learn how to jump."

So begins another brother adventure.

Every year, my three brothers and I have our own summer and winter Olympics. Every Christmas we have the pull-up contest, a Ping-Pong championship (an activity that requires technique and concentration as opposed to brute strength), and a chess competition (to dilute the thirty-weight testosterone). In summer, come hell or high water—accident, bankruptcy, children, divorce, name your picayune excuse—we do an adventure together. It's our opportunity to be back together as brothers, not to mention the chance to revert back to our natural state: drinking, cursing, conferring, deriding, spitting, bragging.

The winter competitions, held as they are in the presence of our spouses, two sisters, parents, children, and other civilized humans sharing holiday cheer, never devolve into sex jokes and debauchery. Not so the summer adventure.

An anthropologist would categorize our ritualized behavior as a primitive form of male bonding. A feminist, in accordance with doctrine, would characterize it as self-destructive machismo. Choose your belief system. There's one thing we know: before we became husbands and fathers, we were brothers. Before all the women who came before our wives or our exes, we were brothers. Before we became what we are, way back when we were chicken-legged prairie boys being knocked around by the Wyoming wind, we were brothers.

Which is not to say that we turned out anything alike. Christopher, the youngest, once a painter, now is a documentary filmmaker in San Francisco. Single, a lover of gorgeous women, he wears a ponytail and an earring and was selected by *Cosmopolitan* magazine as one of the fifty most eligible bachelors in America. Dan, goateed father of two baby girls and a lover of his wife, once owned a gymnastics club; now he is an estimator in the construction business. He lives in Colorado Springs and commutes on a BMW Paris-Dakar motorcycle. Steve, blond, tan, and divorced, with two teenagers, owns his own headhunting firm in Denver, loves country music, and may be the best two-stepper in the city. I live in Wyoming and work in the basement, book-lined scriptorium of an old house full of young females—my wife, two daughters, and a chocolate Lab.

Still, we grew up cheek-to-ruddy-cheek. We share the same blood and the same last name and once shared the same bedrooms. Steve and I, "the big brothers," in one; Dan and Chris, "the little brothers," in the other—wrestling and roughhousing, banging against the walls until we were ordered to take it outside, whence we would tumble into snow or dirt. We rode our bikes right through winter, worked on ranches in summer. We had the last outdoor childhood in America and it branded us. None of us bowl. None of us play cards. None of us golf. None of us have beer guts. We're so barbaric we don't even know who won the World Series or the Super Bowl. We have other vices. Chris is a cliff diver, Dan is a kick boxer, Steve is a cyclist, I climb mountains.

For the past few years our annual misadventure has been a mountain biking/camping trip to the desert from which we unavoidably return scraped, bruised, sunburned, badly hungover, and happy as four boys who've just played hooky. This year time was tight for all of us, threatening our first cancellation, but we refused to forgo tradition. Steve sent out an e-mail: "What about skydiving? Cheap thrills if you ignore the money." Two weeks later, on the weekend Chris turned thirty and Steve turned forty, we were all, once again, together.

The trip got off to an apropos start. Lumbering across the prairie in search of a tiny airstrip in eastern Colorado listening to Taj Mahal croak "She Caught the Katy and Left Me a Mule to Ride," Dan suddenly stops the truck, steps out, and pukes. You might think it's because we'd been up till two A.M. drinking, or you might think it was brought on by the fear of leaping into emptiness thousands of feet above earth, but you don't know Dan. It was stomach flu. I suggest we call it all off but he just wipes his mouth like some Jim Harrison hero.

An hour later we're inside a remote hangar and Woodford is explaining the parts of a parachute.

"Risers, the straps that rise above your shoulders. Control lines, the lines that control the canopy. Steering toggles, the toggles that you use to steer. We skydivers are a simple lot aren't we."

Parachutes aren't what they used to be. The old, round, ungovernable army surplus chutes—the ones you heard of people flying into trees and breaking both legs—are gone. The modern parachute, called a ram-air canopy, is nothing less than an inflatable wing, rectangular in shape and double-layered. As the chute drops through the sky, air is rammed inside nine connected nylon tubes, inflating the canopy like a gigantic air mattress above your head. With judicious use of your steering toggles, you can guide your flight as precisely as a pilot guides a plane. Assuming, of course, that the chute opens.

"Now for malfunctions." Woodford has finished detailing the equipment and how it works, and moved on to how it doesn't.

He pushes in another video. This time a cross-eyed man who apparently takes his fashion inspiration from Charles Manson describes the different ways in which a chute doesn't open. Bag lock—the chute is pulled from the pack but not from its case. Broken lines—the lines connecting your falling body to the life-saving quilt have snapped. Line knots—said lines are tangled and the chute is little more than a fluttering lump. The footage of fouled-up chutes is mesmerizing. When Manson starts to talk about the difference between a partial and a complete malfunction, Woodford pops out the tape.

"Forget that," he says. "You look up and see your chute doing any of that crap, cut away and pull your reserve. There's one thing and only one thing you absolutely must do in skydiving: put a chute above you."

We will get a chance to practice this two-step maneuver, but first he must address another hazard: obstacles.

"Trees, buildings, power lines."

Woodford demonstrates the proper body positions for crashing down through trees and landing on top of buildings.

"But power lines you don't hit, period. Do whatever it takes, turn any direction, hit anything else."

I look down along the table at my three brothers. They all know well the cost of cracking up. You pay to be a participant. The outdoor life is the physical life. Some things heal, some don't, we help each other through. At present, we're all in line for the operating table.

Chris needs surgery on his bottom front teeth. They were snapped out and then pounded back in after getting caught on the wires of a hang glider during a crash landing. Dan needs surgery on his knee after a spectacular snowboarding endo. Steve needs surgery on his left shoulder and left knee, the former the result of an old gymnastics wreck, the latter from a 360 on X-C skis. Last year I dislocated my right shoulder and tore my rotator cuff on a 5.11 off-width.

We move out to a wooden scaffold from which hang parachute harnesses and take turns pulling rip cords for over an hour, constantly giving each other shit.

"Arch one thousand, two one thousand, I can't hear you!" bellows Woodford. "Three one thousand. Four one thousand. Five one thousand. Look up. Bag o' shit. Look down. Punch-right, punch-left!"

We're counting in order to give our chutes a chance to open. We look up to see if the chute is "square." If it is not, if it's a tangled, mortal mess, you look down, grab the red cutaway handle with your right hand, grab the metal reserve handle with your left, take your time, punch-right, punch-left.

Of the thousands of first-time jumpers Woodford has instructed, only two have ever had to pull their reserve. "Both did it just fine," he claims.

But what if you screw up? What if you cut away your main but in the madness of fear, fail to pull your reserve?

"That's what the RSL is for: reserve static line." Woodford shows us a wire that connects the cutaway handle with the reserve chute. "As long as you pull the cutaway handle, the reserve will deploy."

But what if your main chute doesn't open and you're so freaked out you forget everything, go stiff, freeze?

"AAD. Automatic activation device." Woodford shows us a little metal box attached to our harnesses. It measures how fast we're falling. If it's too fast, that is, chutelessly fast, at 2,000 feet above the deck, the AAD will automatically deploy the reserve chute.

There are three kinds of jumps a novice skydiver can make: tandem, AFF, or static line. In a tandem jump, after just twenty minutes of training, you leap from the plane with the instructor attached to you piggyback style. You get a twenty-second free fall before the instructor pulls the ripcord and guides you safely to earth. AFF stands for accelerated free fall. In this jump, following six hours of training, you leap from the plane with two instructors, one on either side of you, again have a twenty-second free fall, but this time you get to pull your own ripcord and steer your own chute. The static line jump is what you see in the old World War II movies. Upon completing four hours of training, you jump from the plane alone and get to steer all alone, but your chute is automatically pulled when you leave the aircraft. No free fall, but no hand-holding.

We chose the static line option. Following the hangar drills, we practiced jumping out of a stationary plane, then practiced landing and rolling, then it was time to go up.

By mutual agreement we would jump in birth order: Mark, Steve, Dan, Chris. As any family psychologist will proclaim, our character is putatively preordained by birth order—the oldest are overachievers, middle children are mediators, youngest children artistic. Perhaps in the beginning, but once we've been adults longer than we were children, the world has kicked us all in the nuts so many times that each of us has hopefully learned how to be all these things. We learn how to walk in our brothers' shoes. Thereafter, the hierarchy collapses, demolishing childhood prejudices. The oldest no longer believe the youngest had it easy; the youngest no longer believe the oldest had it easy. The middle children no longer look up or down to see themselves; they look inside. This is when you start to see what it really means to be a sibling.

We were jumping in birth order only as a nod to our past, to tradition, to a time when we were lined up and our heights cascaded and our hopes swam upstream. Because there were other skydivers, veterans jumping from higher altitudes, we would go up in pairs—Steve and I first, then Dan and Chris, just like old times. The jumpmaster would leap directly after each pair.

Steve and I suited up, plugged on our helmets, and soberly went through the check drills while Dan and Chris made fun of us. That's the job of a brother—to never let you forget who you are or where you came from. The helmets are mounted with radios. After our chutes opened, we would be guided into the drop zone by Woodford, standing with his own radio on the ground. We were to follow his directions precisely and with alacrity.

"You got that?" said Woodford, his voice crackling through the radio, "You listen to me and do exactly what I say."

During the ground course, I think we were all thinking about one another. About the brotherhood. About all the adventures over all the years. About how the adventure was just an excuse for forcing ourselves to re-remember that we were brothers. About how, underneath all the bluster and bravado, having an adventure together was really just a way for guys raised in the stiff-upper-lip tradition to show that we love each other.

I know I was thinking about this when they rolled back the hatch and 3,500 feet of nothingness opened up below me and the jumpmaster was motioning for me to scoot forward and hang my legs out of the plane. I slid my ass over till one cheek was out in midair and I had a death grip on the doorjamb. The wind was blasting in my face and against my body. The jumpmaster smiled and I guess I smiled back. Everything was rushing and the wind and the noise seemed to be flushing through my whole body as if terror were a poison and I tried to calm myself but it wasn't working so I looked out at the wing as we had been drilled to do and jumped.

To say that I was thinking about my brothers in that moment of mortal drop—with the angel plane disappearing above me and the rock-hard ground lunging up beneath me and my entire being feeling like I'd already landed on one of those high-voltage tension lines—would be a magnificent lie. I was scared shitless, bodyless, mindless. For several seconds, the cosmos went blank.

Then the chute opened. Life, precious life, regained!

My lines were crossed so I instinctively reached over my head and drew them apart. I had just completed my canopy control manuevers when Woodford's voice came into my helmet.

"Nice jump, mate. Now I want you to turn right 180 degrees. Good. Now left 180 degrees. Big flare. All right. You're flying!"

It all happened so fast. Three seconds of electrifying terror, then three minutes of God-like, big-perspective, the-world-in-miniature floating.

Woodford was directing me down toward the bull's-eye when I realized something was wrong. I could hear him shouting at Steve.

"Turn right, turn right. No Steve, your other right! Steve, are you listening!"

I landed in a plop and immediately looked up into the sky. I couldn't find Steve. Instead, the jumpmaster was twirling in fast, touching down beside me.

"He's lost his helmet!" shouted the jumpmaster. "Use the arrow!"

Woodford scrambled to unfurl a large fabric arrow on the ground, an emergency device used to guide jumpers who have lost radio contact. Steve had tumbled out of the plane and the static line had caught around his head and ripped off his helmet.

Chris, Dan, and I were all standing there together staring up into the blue sky at one brother, hoping with one heart. Our fear was that he was unconscious—just floating in the welkin like a limp doll—and would crash-land into power lines, a barbed wire fence, a highway. He could break his back, snap his neck, impale himself . . .

But though he was a long way off, it was clear he was in control, unassisted yet unpanicked. He was directing his chute toward the drop zone.

In a couple minutes, Steve landed softly out in the prairie.

Later, Chris and Dan would execute their jumps flawlessly—Dan, lime green but holding back vomit because they won't let you jump if you're puking; Chris naturally hitting the bull's-eye and winning the bet—both dives sadly undramatic.

It's hard to describe how you feel when a brother is in peril. For a moment, your soul enters his and you are there beside him, with him, holding his hand. On any ordinary day four sanguine brothers like us wouldn't be caught dead holding hands.

Only on an adventure.

From the Mouths of Babes

The last time I saw Coach his body was puffy. His chiseled face was unchanged—flat lips, deep eyes, dark hair, still handsome as the young Clint Eastwood—but he looked as if he were wearing someone else's inflated, definitionless body.

The disease had progressed that far. I was at the top of a climb with several friends when he appeared at the base of the smooth granite wall. It struck me as strange to see him just standing there on the ground rather than climbing.

All of us up on the ledge had once been his athletes. Coach had led us and the rest of the Laramie High School swim team to seven consecutive state championship titles. He was a man at once compassionate, taciturn, and merciless. Every day for years Coach got us to swim till our bodies turned to lead—till our legs couldn't move and our arms couldn't come out of the water. He made the strongest swim 400, 500, 600 laps. Some of these laps were fifty-yard sprints against the clock. They were almost unbearable, and yet we did it. Coach constantly, if often wordlessly, pushed us to go faster, try harder. We never complained, but everybody thought this was outrageous, because everybody thought we were only training for the state meet—except Coach. He knew the meet would come and go and then we'd graduate and the trophies would disappear into boxes and what he'd helped make of us would be all that was left.

Besides commanding the swim team, he'd taught PE classes in swimming, karate (he was a black belt, naturally), and rock climbing. Karate demanded too much quiet discipline for most of us hormone-fueled jocks, and more swimming was out of the question, so we signed up for rock climbing. Every morning until the mountains were buried in snow, Coach drove the bus up to the rocks in the dark so we would be climbing by dawn and back to school by second period. In the biting mornings of late fall and early spring our fingers would become so numb we could hardly feel the rock.

That was a decade and a half ago. Now Coach was staring up at us, squinting into the sun. It was a gorgeous Wyoming autumn afternoon: not a cloud, not a breath of wind, air crisp as kindling. We shouted down, asking him if he'd brought his rock shoes along. He shook his head but then motioned for us to lower the rope. We glanced at each other. We were at the top of Fall Wall, an infamous 5.10 route composed of nothing but tiny eighth-inch holds, the kind that require precise edging with tight rock shoes. Coach was in running shoes, with no harness.

When the rope reached him he picked up the end, tied it around his waist with a bowline, looked up, and yelled, "On belay?"

In the beginning, Coach had taught us how to climb without a harness as well—how to just wrap the rope around your waist several times, tie a knot called the bowline-on-a-coil, and go. It was the mid-1970s. In Wyoming, the ethics of climbing were still largely descendant from mountaineering, as were the techniques and the gear. We climbed on ropes stiff as lariats using aluminum nuts and iron pitons for protection. Knowing your knots mattered. Route finding mattered. A climber of conscience climbed only what he could lead in good style. No hangs, no falls, no excuses. I never saw Coach climb any other way. It was a matter of pride, of character. Today people climb harder, but not bolder.

"Belay on!" I answered.

And Coach started to climb.

The moment he touched the rock his bloated, betrayed body was transformed. It was as though he had stepped into a world without gravity. He climbed with utter silence and grace. Each movement was discrete and intentional and yet he seemed to flow up the wall, like water in reverse. Every foot placement was sure and confident and his feet stuck to the rock like glue. It didn't matter that his sloppy shoes couldn't possibly use the tiny edges. *If you believe your feet will stick, they'll stick.* That's what Coach used to tell us when we were halfway up a climb and our feet started slipping and we started whining.

I made my first lead with Coach. I'd only done three or four climbs when he handed me two pieces of gear and pointed up to a 5.7 off-width called Upper Slot. I put in both pieces of protection low on the climb, got about twenty feet above the second piece, and froze. Too scared to go up, incapable of climbing down, I hung there like a frightened kitten. Coach watched and waited. After a while I started to tremble, then shake. Soon fear had taken over so completely I was shuddering. Coach yelled at me to get my head together and just finish the climb, but by now I had already lost my head. I was puling shamelessly and fatigue was sickening me and I was losing my grip and my feet were slipping off. I was certain I was going to fall and die ignominiously when Coach soloed up behind me. Standing steady as a solid platform right under my feet, he handed up a fist-size piece of protection, a #11 hexentric, and told me in a calm, stern voice to put it in and climb to the top, which I did.

Twenty-five years of climbing and I have never been as scared since. For a long time I thought he had been cruel, because I thought Coach was merely trying to teach me how to rock-climb, how to be a rock climber. But most of Coach's students never became rock climbers. I'm sure he didn't expect they would. They would forget the skill but perhaps remember the will.

That autumn afternoon, Coach climbed Fall Wall as fluidly as a dancer. He did it in worn-out running shoes with a body that was no longer his. Unlike every other coach I ever had, and for that matter almost any person I've met, Coach was a man who expected more from himself than from you. When he got to the top he didn't say a word. He momentarily flashed his Man With No Name smile. I never saw him again.

Coach Layne Kopishka died of hemochromatosis—a disease in which there is too much iron in the blood—on July 11, 1992, just a few months after my first daughter was born. He left behind a wife, Judy, and two daughters, Shawna and Tonya. Coach was forty-seven.

Not long ago I started trying to teach my daughters how to rock-climb. At the time, Addi was six and Teal was three.

We didn't go to the climbing gym. My girls like playing on the artificial wall, but when you're in a box with a roof rather than outside beneath the sky, surrounded by walls instead of horizons and fluorescent light instead of sunshine, you learn very different things. We went into the mountains, to a dome of rounded pink granite named the Rat Brain, not far from Upper Slot and Fall Wall.

There were six of us in all, if you count Meggie our chocolate Lab: Addi and Teal, Justin Moe, me, and my friend Ed, a philosophy professor who has more patience and compassion than I do, which is why I recruit him for instructional adventures.

Stepping out of the truck we were blasted by a cold wind and everyone donned wool caps and windbreakers. We had backpacks, water bottles, apples, climbing harnesses, locking carabiners, and belay devices. Addi brought along her books, Justin brought his ratty down jacket, Teal brought her stuffed seal.

The path along the top of the beaver dam where we usually crossed the creek was flooded, so we had to search for another route across. The kids ran upstream and discovered a game trail through a meadow that leapt the creek and wove on through the willows. Above the creek we discovered a lean-to hidden in the aspens: fallen logs angled against a boulder blackened from a fire pit. Addi, Justin, and Teal wanted to stay and play, but I insisted they keep moving.

(Just a note: One of the many ridiculous maxims that have been whirling about in Dadland since the late 1960s is, Never push or pull

your child. Let your child do exactly what she wants and she'll naturally rise to her potential. Spare me. We all push and pull our kids; the
questions are how, when, and to what degree.)

On the lower slabs of rock beyond the trees, I had to hand the
kids up to Ed at several difficult places, but Meggie, a rock dog who's
been going into the mountains with me since she was three months
old, used her clawed paws like a double set of crampons, forcefully
scratching her way up. A climbing buddy of mine swears he's seen
Meggie do a pull-up.

This was our second outing. We'd all come to the Rat Brain a week
before and it had turned into a battlefield where Ed and I suffered an
ignoble defeat: the kids had started whimpering, saying they didn't
like rock climbing and refusing to continue. Teal had bounced back
the very next day, asking when we would get to go back. (Being three,
I think she was enthralled by the name Rat Brain.) A few days later
Justin left a message on my office phone machine asking to go climbing again. But Addi, an intellectual at six, would not let the rosy light
of nostalgia color her harsh experience. The only way I got her to go
a second time was by promising her that she didn't have to climb
unless she wanted to. Hence the books stuffed in her pack alongside
her harness. She could read while Justin and Teal climbed.

When we arrived at the base of the Rat Brain it was so windy the
kids were getting knocked over. Teal, Justin, and Addi hid behind a
boulder with their noses running. Even Ed admitted it was cold. But
soon enough they got themselves occupied. Justin checked out "the
bathtub"—an erosion hollow in the rock filled with snowmelt—for
insects. I could see none but he of course found loads. Justin is a born
naturalist. Addi sat down, got out her books, and began to read,
grasping the pages tightly so they wouldn't flap. Teal started playing
with the carabiners, linking them together like paper clips. None of
them was the least bit interested in climbing.

Nonetheless, Ed scaled the cerebrum of the Rat Brain and clipped in the ropes while I got each of the kids into their harnesses. They ignored me, moving their arms and legs automatically while continuing to play or read. I asked Justin if he wanted to go first; he said he'd rather continue plucking bugs out of the mud. I reminded him that he had called me to go climbing.

"Ohhh-kaayy." He stood up, heaved his narrow shoulders, and jiggled the rope indifferently.

I belayed while Ed soloed beside Justin, giving moral support, pointing out handholds and footholds, and demonstrating the proper body position for face climbing. Justin's gym shoes were too big and they peeled off halfway up. He had to be lowered in his socks and Ed secured the shoes on his feet by wrapping them with athletic tape. After that he climbed well, if slowly, pretending to be scared but concentrating. At the top he threw his arms into the cold blue sky and let out a whoop.

Teal was next. Ed belayed, I climbed alongside. She never looked back, or down for that matter. She was soon to turn four—as she told everyone—and considered herself the equal of any six-year-old. Ignoring my advice on where to put her feet and which handholds to hang on to, simply assuming her little feet inside her little tennis shoes would stay wherever she placed them, she scampered straight to the top. I showed her how to throw her hands in the air like Justin, and she did it, but she didn't get it. Climbing up a cold rock face in wind that could lift her off her feet just wasn't that big a deal. On the other hand, she throws her hands in the air all the time when we put on music in the living room. She loves to dance.

There are purportedly dads who still believe teaching is a one-way street. You preach, they pray. In fact, you learn immediately that teaching is a wide, two-way boulevard with lots of crazy traffic, ideas and education zooming in both directions. If you're teaching a kid, then the kid is teaching you back.

Addi knew I had promised her I wouldn't force her, but she also knew I wouldn't leave her alone. She gave in after repeated coaxing. Ed belayed and I coached. Up on the rock her genuine fear of heights reasserted itself. She was only five feet off the ground when her legs began to tremble. She tried to move up and her feet slipped and her fingernails dug desperately into the rock. She was on the verge of tears. I felt like a shit.

"Addi, calm down." I had my hand on her back. "Look for something to put your feet on." I pointed out two small dishes in the rock.

She listened. She focused. She placed the toes of her hiking boots on the slopey concavities and her body relaxed slightly.

"All right! See that?"

She gave me a grim smile. She kept climbing, but she didn't go all the way to the top. At the start she had told me that she would climb to the second bolt and no further. I'd told her that when she got that high she would want to keep going. She didn't. She wanted to come down. Still, when she got back on the ground she was beaming.

Justin agreed to tie in again only if I promised to watch over the cup of bugs he had collected. He was planning to bring them home to show his mom. I obviously didn't understand the value of insects, so he didn't trust me: while he was climbing he kept looking down to make sure his bugs were safe.

When I asked Teal if she wanted to climb again she lightheartedly said no. Then seconds later, just as gaily, she said yes. She roped in and flitted up the wall and came down and went back to reorganizing my spare carabiners.

Addi, inspired by her first success, climbed to the second bolt again, but even with urging wouldn't go higher. She came down and went back to reading.

While Ed and I coiled the ropes the kids ate their apples and drank from their water bottles and wiped their noses and stared out across the frigid mountains. The truck was a mile away and we raced back, Ed and I getting them all to run to stay warm. They each took several rough tumbles in the woods before we reached the truck. We piled in, I cranked up the heat, and we began grinding homeward along the jeep road.

Once we were back on the highway, after everyone was warm and before the knock-knock jokes started, I asked our three small climbers if they could tell me one thing that they'd learned. It could only be one thing, the most important thing.

They sat quietly for a moment, thinking. I expected them to say something technical about rock climbing—"Don't hug the rock" or "Don't use your knees" or "Look for footholds"—one of the rules Ed and I had exposited.

Justin was resting his head on Ed's shoulder. He looked subdued, a rare state for a boy like Justin, but then he screwed up his face, his cheeks suddenly red as cherries, and shouted, "Move swiftly!"

I looked at Teal. She already had her answer. She threw her hands in the air and yelled, "Don't whine!"

Addi, glowing with pride, quietly said, "Try your hardest."

Ed slapped his thighs.

The next day Ed, the philosopher, told me he had gone home, written their lessons down, and taped them on his wall.

Move swiftly. Don't whine. Try your hardest.

If Coach were still alive I would have written him a letter and told him this story. But then he already knew it.

About the Author

Mark Jenkins lives in Laramie, Wyoming, with his wife and two daughters. Formerly the investigative editor for Men's Health, he is now a columnist for Outside magazine. His writing has also appeared in GQ, Playboy, Condé Nast Traveler, Backpacker, Reader's Digest, and The Washington Post.

CPSIA information can be obtained at www.ICGtesting.com
Printed in the USA
LVOW102300160712

290360LV00001B/62/A

9 780743 249416